EDWARD HARRINGTON

SELECTED VERSE

BSB
BLADE SHED BOOKS

This collection first published in 2026 by Blade Shed Books

Poems by Edward Phillip Harrington (1895–1966)

This edition and introduction © David Williams 2026

Every effort has been made to trace copyright holders and to obtain their permission for the use of material. The publisher makes no claim to copyright in the original poems and would be grateful if notified of any information regarding rights holders by contacting info@bladeshedbooks.au. Any omissions or errors will be corrected in future printings.

Blade Shed Books
www.bladeshedbooks.au

A catalogue record for this book is available from
the National Library of Australia.

ISBN 978 1 76434 240 7

Front cover portrait *Ted Harrington* by Charles Salis Lloyd,
courtesy State Library Victoria
Back cover and title page photograph of Edward Harrington
courtesy State Library of Queensland
Cover and text design by Sandra Nobes
Set in 10½pt Adobe Garamond

1 3 5 7 9 10 8 6 4 2

Contents

Introduction	vi
An Embarkation Song	1
An Outpost	3
The Desert	6
The Photo	9
Lone Pine	13
In the Ward	15
The Hills of Whroo	18
A Cry from the City	21
The Birds	24
The Cripple's New Year's Eve	28
Boundary Bend	30
Thirty-Five	33
The Ballad of Mick O'Bree	36
Shylock Revised	43
A Little Bit of Land	49
A Cry from the Mallee	51
Pulling Teats	53
On the Rail of the Bar	57
Lightning	61
The Old Blade Shed	63
Not To-day	66
Cats on the Roof	68
Retrospect	70
Memories	72

Billy Woods	75
If Morgan Knew	80
By the Wady Imelaga	84
The Brothers O'Brien	87
Song of the Sinai	91
The Mother Speaks	94
The Dead Come Home	96
Throwing Pebbles in the Sea	99
My Garden of Golden Dreams	103
A Random Shaft	105
The Girl in the Street	107
Pedigree	109
Socrates	111
Slander	115
Cradle Song	116
The Quiet Folk	117
The Kerrigan Boys	119
The Bushrangers	125
My Old Black Billy	127
The Tarra Valley	128
The Red Steer	129
Drover's Song	131
The Fossicker	133
Old Timer	134
The Girl of the Range	136
"There's Only Two of Us Here"	137
The Swagman's Song	139
Lasseter's Last Long Ride	140

Banjo	142
Port Noarlunga	145
The Derelicts	146
O'Brien's Leap	150
The Girl with the Pram	152
The Lame Fiddler	154
The Last of the Kellys	156
Lords of the Weddin Range	158
The Ghost of Ben Hall	160
Morgan	162
Guinan	164
Insomnia	169
Brunette and Blonde	172
Blood on the Rose	174
"Gentlemen, the Press!"	175
The Swagless Swaggie	178
Spooks and Spirits	182
Brady	185
Mallacoota	187
Winds of the Wilderness	189
Ballad of Discontent	190
End of a Joyous Bard	193
Requiem	196
Acknowledgements	199

Introduction

Even in his lifetime, Edward Harrington's books were hard to come by. In a 1955 feature for *Overland* magazine, novelist Frank Hardy wrote, "I have never been able to get hold of a copy of *Songs of War and Peace*," which was published in 1920.[1] Harrington's 1936 *Boundary Bend and Other Ballads* sold out within two months and became "almost impossible to procure".[2] There's a report that suggests stocks of his 1944 *The Kerrigan Boys and Other Australian Verses* were lost in a warehouse fire.[3] His last published collection, *The Swagless Swaggie and Other Ballads*, was published in 1957 and is difficult to find. For fifty years from 1916, most readers found Edward "Ted" Harrington's poems in copies of *The Bulletin*, *Overland*, *Bohemia* or *The Labor Call*.

Born in Shepparton in 1895, Ted was one of eight children raised on family farms at Pine Lodge, Bunbartha and Colbinabbin. Reflecting on his childhood in a 1955 interview with Stephen and Anita Murray-Smith, Ted recalled he finished school when he was about thirteen. He explained, "I never went to school much at all, really. The old man couldn't afford to let me go to school. We had to do the work on the farm."[4] His bitterly funny poem "Pulling Teats" captures those childhood experiences:

> I was reared on a selection; I'm a product of the land,
> For my old man had a dairy and we milked the cows by hand.
> ...
> Oh, my youth was sadly blighted, and my young dreams went to bits
> While those precious hours I wasted in the cow-shed pulling teats!

Ted Harrington has been described as the "last of the bush balladists", a "successor of Lawson and Paterson".[5] In the Murray-Smith interview, Ted describes how he was first influenced by the classic English poets including Campbell, Scott, Burns and Wordsworth. "I wasn't much interested in Henry Lawson or Banjo Paterson or E.J. Brady prior to going away to the 1914 war. All my early works in *Songs of War and Peace* were based on the standard works in England. I had no sense of an Australian sentiment. But over in the Light Horse, after the Charge of Beersheba—well, I found out we were a nation. I started to write Australian." Ted traced the basis of much of his work to his father and the tales he would tell around the campfire. "My father had a wonderful fund of old bush stories. He was a good old yarn spinner."[6]

Ted's verses had a quality that allowed them to enter folk tradition. In the early 1950s, when playwright Dick Diamond was searching for authentic Australian folk songs for his new musical *Reedy River*, he attended a party at which a former shearer sang a song he'd learned in the shearing sheds called "My Old Black Billy". It was perfect for Diamond's purposes, capturing the spirit of the old swagmen. And so "My Old Black Billy" became the hit song of his show. What many took for a traditional folk song was, in fact, a modern ballad: Ted wrote the verses in 1938 and Roy Jefferies set them to music in 1940. It took some time before the original version was discovered.[7] As Frank Hardy wrote: "In fifteen years, it established itself as a folk song; a most unusual feat."[8]

While he wrote memorable and popular bush ballads, one critic argued that "it is as a 'Digger poet' that he is at his strongest."[9] Ted enlisted on 22 February 1917 aged twenty-one and was posted to the 4th Light Horse Brigade. He would recall, "I was only in camp for six weeks. I think it was exactly three months from the time I joined [to when] I got to the front line. They didn't mess about then." He took part in the famous mounted Charge at Beersheba on 31 October 1917 and in operations in the Jordan Valley where his mate, Bill Woods, was killed in action. Ted's poems about war and its impacts stand out. His elegy "Billy Woods" is a fine example.

> At the break of day I sought you and I found you lying there
> With the red blood on your tunic, and the red sand in your hair;
> Lying just as you had fallen, and I knelt and pressed your hand—
> Oh! the hopes, the dreams, the longings that lie buried in the sand!
>
> Now the war is long since over, and I'm tramping in the West,
> And I sometimes think, old comrade, after all you fared the best.
> You are better off than I am in your far-off desert grave,
> For a man must tramp for tucker in the land he fought to save.

After returning from the war in 1919 Ted said he tried the plasterer's trade in Melbourne and spent some time in South Australia. He also helped his father pioneer a farm near Boundary Bend in the Mallee region of Victoria, which suffered severe droughts during the 1920s and '30s. His poem "A Cry from the Mallee" captures the hope and hardship of that venture.

> And this is the harvest of all our hopes, the fruits of our simple trust:
> A stretch of barren and wind-swept slopes that redden the skies with dust;
> And this is the measure of all we've won from seasons of ceaseless work—
>
> But, sooner or later, the drought must break, and the seasons change again,
> We still have faith though our hearts may ache—and we'll battle along till then.

Despite their determination, the battle was lost. A succession of droughts sent them broke and they had to "walk off the farm".[10]

In 1936, Ted settled in North Melbourne and remained there. He worked at the Department of Aircraft Production from 1942 until he received a pension for ill health in around 1954.[11] He was active in literary circles and societies and championed the legacies of Adam Lindsay Gordon, Henry Lawson and Banjo Paterson. Ted became good friends with many writers including E.J. Brady and John Shaw Neilson. Brady lived in Mallacoota and Ted visited on many occasions, inspiring his poem "Mallacoota".

> I have always loved the forest,
>   I have always loved the sea;
> Now here at Mallacoota
>   Both my loves are close to me.
> I can feel their mighty pulses,
>   I can hear their great hearts beat
> With the forest close behind me
>   And the ocean at my feet.

Ted enjoyed many enduring friendships, but he never married or had children. Reflecting on his work at the age of sixty, he said one of his favourite poems was "Thirty-Five".[12] 'We've very few illusions left when we are thirty-five,' he told Hardy.[13]

> I might have married years ago; I should have done in fact.
> I loved the girl and she loved me; 'twas courage that I lacked.
> That sad night haunts my mem'ry still, the night when last
>   we kissed.
> I bitterly regret at times the happiness I missed;
> But all that now is past and done: 'tis useless to revive
> The tender dreams of twenty-one when we are thirty-five.

Ted died in May 1966 at his home in North Melbourne, aged seventy. Despite decades of scarcity of his books, Ted Harrington remains well-known and loved among Australian poetry and folk music enthusiasts. His legacy has endured for more than a century because his work captures authentic Australian stories, sentiments and settings: the farm, the war, the Mallee, the city, friendship, loss and the compromises we make with our dreams.

This new collection, the first in nearly seventy years, solves two problems: the decades-old difficulty of getting one's hands on a copy of an Edward Harrington book, and the uncertainty of his legacy—a challenge Frank Hardy posed when he wrote, "In any event, many of Ted's songs and verses will live on through the years to come. Some would contest this, certainly Ted himself would—but then neither Edward Harrington nor his 'cultured critics' will decide the issue, future generations of Australians will."[14] With this publication, the issue has been decided: Ted's verses will live on for many more years.

DAVID J WILLIAMS

Notes:

1. Frank Hardy, "Edward Harrington", *Overland*, no. 3 (Autumn 1955): 3–6.
2. "A Mallee Poet", *Ouyen Mail*, 23 June 1937, 4 (Trove digitised newspaper); "Poets' Portraits", *The Age*, 5 June 1937, 7 (Trove digitised newspaper); "A 'Digger' Poet—Work of Edward Harrington", *The Age*, 26 April 1952, 10 (Trove digitised newspaper).
3. Florence Hagelüken, "Vale Ted Harrington", *Bohemia* 15, no. 9 (July 1966): 1–2.
4. Edward Harrington, interview by Stephen Murray-Smith and Nita Murray-Smith, 1955, sound recording, Alan Scott Folklore Collection, State Library of Victoria.
5. Frank E. Blake, introduction to *The Swagless Swaggie and other ballads: selected verse of Edward Harrington*, by Edward Harrington (Melbourne: Australasian Book Society, 1957); advertisement for *The Kerrigan Boys and Other Australian Verses*, *Central Queensland Herald* (Rockhampton, Qld), 22 February 1945, 10 (Trove digitised newspaper).
6. Harrington, interview by Murray-Smith and Murray-Smith, 1955.
7. *Reedy River Songbook* (Sydney: New Theatre, 1954), note to "My Old Black Billy"; reproduced in Bush Music Club, "From the Archives—How the 'Anonymous Folk Song' My Old Black Billy Came to Be in Reedy River", August 2019.
8. Hardy, "Edward Harrington", 3.
9. "A 'Digger' Poet", *The Age*, 26 April 1952 (Trove digitised newspaper).
10. Harrington, interview by Murray-Smith and Murray-Smith, 1955.
11. Ibid.
12. Ibid.
13. Hardy, "Edward Harrington", 4.
14. Ibid.

An Embarkation Song

The drums beat loud, the banners fly, we're going aboard to-day,
The transports, and the convoys, too, wait ready in the bay,
A cruel despot's lust for power has plunged the world in wrath,
And England sounds the call to arms, and sends her bravest forth.
We rally swiftly to her aid, we need no spur nor goad,
But march breast-forward to the fray, down duty's open road;
Our star-crossed banner floats above, we'll keep it free from stain
Till we come back, till we come back, till we come back again.

But think not lightly from our homes and all we love we part,
We know the land we leave behind holds many an aching heart,
And as our good ship cleaves the foam, and as our shores grow dim,
There's many a soldier's heart will grieve for those who weep for him.
There'll be a gap in many a home, that time may never fill,
But though our homes are dear to us, there's something dearer still,
And should Britannia need our lives, her glory to maintain,
We won't come back, we won't come back, we won't come back again,

For Fate at last has struck the hour, and we must stand the test,
A mighty cause must be upheld, a nation's wrongs redressed;
On wasted Europe's trampled turf we yet must prove our steel,
On many a crimson battle-plain our faith we'll redly seal:
We'll show how Austral sons can fight—and die, should need arise,
To guard their sunny Southern land, the fairest 'neath the skies;
Till right shall triumph over wrong, and peace and freedom reign,
We won't come back, we won't come back, we won't come back again.

Our comrades need us badly now, we will not shirk nor stay,
Our star-crossed banner floats above, and lights us on our way;
'Twill float ere long 'midst shot and shell, where Britain's bravest are,
'Twill light us on to victory's shrine, a constant guiding star.
So now farewell to those we love, one last and lingering kiss,
And if we don't return to you, sweethearts, remember this:
That honour's noblest roll is death, thrice blest will be the slain,
Who won't come back, who won't come back, who won't come back again.

An Outpost

Mother, to-night I am lying
    Under the steadfast stars,
Save for the night-wind sighing,
    Nothing the silence mars.
Below me the Dead Sea glistens,
    Like a silver shield in the gloom,
And away in the hazy distance
    The mountains of Moab loom.

My comrades are wrapped in slumber,
    Their rifles beside them laid,
While I watch, in the silence sombre,
    Striving to pierce the shade;
For I know, though the stars are gleaming
    And the crescent moon shines clear,
In the shadows so peaceful seeming,
    Danger and death lurk near.

Often, on outpost duty,
    When the heavens are sown with stars,
And night with its purple beauty,
    Has hidden the crags and scars,
Musing o'er memories pleasant,
    Homeward my fancies range,
Till the past seems the real present,
    And the present unreal and strange.

Do the reeds still sway by the river?
    Do the wattles break in the bend,
Where the song of the bell-birds ever
    With the murmur of waters blend?

To the northward, a searchlight gleaming
    Like a great sword severs the sky,
And I wake again from my dreaming
    Of the halcyon days gone by.

It may be a fancy only
    Born of a bitter mood,
But o'er these mountains lonely
    A heaviness seems to brood;
A something, vague and uncanny,
    Tragic, yet undefined,
Haunting each crag and cranny,
    Pregnant in ev'ry wind.

Oh, grim and forbidding ranges,
    Grey from the storms of years,
Watching through all its changes
    This drama of blood and tears;
Sombre and sad and massive,
    Like sentinels stern and dumb,
Ye have watched through the years impassive,
    And shall watch through the years to come.

But the winds of the dawn are waking,
    And, away, in the east afar
The mystical day is breaking
    Under the morning star.
So soon may this night of sorrow
    Melt and dissolve away,
While the bells of a glad to-morrow
    Proclaim a brighter day.

The Desert

The red sun sinks o'er the sand-waste, the cares of the day
    are dead,
Softly across the desert the mantle of night is spread,
While I lie on the warm sand, dreaming, vaguely depressed
    in mind,
As my thoughts flit back to the homeland and the friends
    I have left behind.

Oh! the trail that lies before us is a long and a lonely one,
Our faces are turned to the desert, and our journey has
    scarce begun;
But we'll face the future undaunted, whatever it holds in
    store,
And we'll do our best for the old land, like the lads who
    have gone before.

Here, in this desolate country, fever and famine cursed,
We are camped on a dreary desert, whose thirst is a
    quenchless thirst;
Day by day we are drilling under the sun's fierce glare,
Dust in our mouth and nostrils, dust in our eyes and hair.

Each day has a dreary sameness, the sun, the wind, and the
    sand,
Nothing can ever vary in this strange and desolate land;
Ever away in the distance the pitiless heat-waves dance,
Till the eye grows weary of gazing over its vast expanse.

It may be delusions only, a vision of tired eyes,
But oft, when the winds are whirling, and the eddying sand-clouds rise,
I seem to see in the distance armies ghostly and grand,
With banners and pennons waving, marching across the sand.

Often, mayhap, unknowing, with measured and muffled tread,
We pass over buried cities, that were great in the ages dead;
Over tower and rampart, over spire and dome,
Centres of ancient commerce, older than Greece or Rome.

They were proud in their day of splendour, deeming themselves secure,
They fashioned their walls and temples with a strength that would aye endure;
Ever they toiled and builded, ever their wealth increased,
Still richer the Royal raiment, and richer the Royal feast.

But nearer, and ever nearer, while the sentinels waked or slept,
To the walls of the frowning ramparts an unseen foeman crept;
Ever nearer and nearer, till their glory was overthrown.
And the desert had closed above them, claiming them as her own.

Well, p'raps she will claim us also, hushing our hearts to rest,
Spreading her mantle o'er us, clasping us to her breast;
Many of Britain's bravest under her sand-wastes lie,
Around them the great grey desert, above them the star- sown sky.

But night, like a dusky garment, closer around me clings.
And I seem to hear in the heavens the fanning of unseen wings;
Straining my ears, I listen for the call of some lone night bird,
But never a shadow passes, never a sound is heard.

Now the great white moon is rising, queenly and calm and sweet,
Shedding her radiance tender, and the bugle sounds retreat;
The night winds whisper around me, soothing my troubled mind,
Seeming to whisper softly, "The desert is not unkind."

Ah! well, good-bye to the old life, good-bye to the olden dreams,
Our faces are turned to the sand-waste, where the mocking mirage gleams;
But we'll follow the path of duty, and we will not falter nor fail,
Till we rest from our toil and sorrow, at the end of the long, long trail.

The Photo

I sit alone in my darkened room,
    Sad and sombre, my thoughts and I,
The old clock ticks through the tense grey gloom,
    Like the tramp of a regiment marching by.

Yet not alone—from the walls above
    Ghostly faces stare down at me,
Faces I've loved, and faces I love,
    Playmates and friends of the used-to-be.

But one there is, from the rest apart,
    Whose dark eyes follow me to and fro,
Peering into my very heart,
    Waking echoes of long ago.

The eyes of a soldier, who never quailed
    When the country woke to the bugle call,
He sent me a token before he sailed—
    The photo. that stares from the darkened wall.

Oh! the sun shines bright on the dewy lawn,
    The swallow is tending her noisy brood,
But, ah! my curtains are closely drawn,
    No cheerful sunbeam may here intrude.

For sad as death is my heart to-day,
    And this quiet chamber to me is dear;
I am dreaming of one who is far away,
    Yet who in spirit seems lingering near.

Tender thoughts of the olden times,
    Happy days that were all too brief;
Stealing o'er me like far, faint chimes,
    Fill my bosom with poignant grief.

Down by the creek, where we loved to roam,
    Stood the gaunt old gum that our father rung,
Where an eagle had chosen to build her home,
    And season by season to rear her young.

Oh! that fierce old eagle, I ween, was shrewd,
    She had built her nest on a wide-flung arm
Of the ancient gum, where she reared her brood
    Unmolested, and free from harm.

Oft of a morn, as we passed below,
    We would pause to ponder and speculate
As to whether the eagle had eggs or no,
    But the limb was feeble, the height was great.

Yes, the limb was weak, and you wondered oft
    If under your weight it would bend or crack,
And you measured the fall, as you gazed aloft,
    With the practised eye of a steeplejack.

But you put the matter to test at length,
>   As the only way to dispel the doubt;
You ventured all on the old limb's strength,
>   And spat on your hands, and went crawling out.

Lord! I recall how my senses reeled,
>   How my blood ran cold, and my eyes grew dim;
The fierce old eagle above you wheeled
>   As you held your way on that crazy limb.

Just once you paused, with a backward look,
>   But the nest was near, and you set your teeth;
How the eagle screamed! how the old limb shook!
>   Till my heart stood still as I watched beneath.

But the Fates were kind, and, without mishap,
>   You got the eggs—what a grand reward!
With one in your mouth, and two in your cap,
>   You landed safe on the sunlit sward.

Thus, ever reckless of life and limb,
>   Whether climbing high for a few frail shells
Or swimming where others would fear to swim,
>   Or storming a ridge in the Dardanelles.

Always fearless, and free, and frank,
>   Never by hardship or risk appalled;
Always found in the foremost rank,
>   Whenever duty or danger called.

Alas! those dreams of the days long dead,
>   How soon they summon the scalding tears!
Memory gathers each broken thread,
>   Busily bridging the void of years.

Eyes, unseeing, that gaze in mine,
>   Lifelike lips, that are always dumb,
Will ye shine again as ye used to shine?
>   Will ye speak again in the years to come?

I cannot say, I can but hope on,
>   Through all the years I will wait and yearn;
Only one of the thousands gone,
>   Thousands of whom will no more return.

But the call of duty must be obeyed,
>   'Tis weak to weep, and 'tis vain to sigh,
Many already the price have paid,
>   Dying grimly, as heroes die.

Eternal glory to those who fall,
>   Faithful and true, on the shell-torn sod,
Giving for freedom their lives—their all,
>   Yielding their spirits again to God.

Lone Pine

Lone Pine! Lone Pine! our hearts are numbly aching
    For those who come no more,
Our boys who sleep the sleep that knows no waking,
    Beside the Dardans' shore.
Through all the years, with glory sad and sombre,
    Their names will deathless shine;
No bugle call can wake them from their slumber:
    Lone Pine! Lone Pine!

They did not quail, they did not pause or ponder,
    They counted not the odds;
The order came, the foe were waiting yonder,
    The rest was with the gods.
Forth from their trenches at the signal leaping,
    They charged the Turkish line,
And Death charged, too, a royal harvest reaping,
    Lone Pine! Lone Pine!

Naught could withstand that onrush, backward driven,
    The foemen broke and fled,
Abandoning the trenches, wrecked and riven,
    The dying and the dead.
Night fell upon that scene of sombre glory,
    Beside the murmuring brine,
But few, alas! were left to tell the story,
    Lone Pine! Lone Pine!

The guns are hushed, that grim adventure ended,
    The dead are lying low;
Australia rises, resolute and splendid,
    Triumphant o'er the foe.
But thou, grim field, whose fruit was bitter failure,
    Deep in our hearts we'll shrine
Thy name, forever sacred to Australia,
    Lone Pine! Lone Pine!

In the Ward

The lamps were shaded, no sound was heard
    In the silent ward, where the wounded lay,
Save when a patient moaned and stirred,
    Or a footstep echoed and died away.

Here, in this chamber, so sad and still,
    Haggard of feature and faint of breath,
Languid and low, lay the maimed and ill,
    In the shadowy valley 'twixt life and death.

But lo! a glimmer of light is seen,
    A rustle of skirts, and a gentle tread,
A white-robed sister, with furtive mien,
    Passes, flitting from bed to bed.

She pauses softly, with tender grace,
    Beside the bed of a wounded man,
The lamplight gleams on his haggard face,
    Ghastly pallid beneath the tan.

An Anzac soldier, wide-eyed and wan,
    He stared at her with a vacant stare,
With fevered brilliance his dark eyes shone,
    But reason's light was no longer there.

She smoothed his pillow, she stroked his brow,
    Did he feel the touch of her soft, cool hand?
She wondered. What was he dreaming now,
    This long, lean son of the great South land?

Where were his thoughts—in the crowded trench?
    Did he stand once more 'midst the maimed and dead,
Rifle in hand, 'midst the heat and stench,
    The thunder of guns and the hiss of lead?

No! for the smile on his face betrayed
    No hint of sorrow, no thought of strife,
Back o'er the ocean his thoughts had strayed,
    Back to the scenes of his early life.

Back to the bush that he knew and loved,
    The great grey bush that was free to all,
Where, light of heart, he had roamed and roved
    Ere he sailed to answer the War God's call.

To ceaseless striving with flood and drought,
    To lonely rides o'er the hazy plains,
To saving stock when the floods were out,
    And the rivers swollen by winter rains.

To the old, free life on the runs outback,
    Where ev'ry man was a rider born,
To moonlit rides o'er the mountain track,
    To rattling gallops at early morn.

To merry meetings of old and young,
    In the old bush homes, in the nights gone by,
Where the fiddles squeaked, and the dancers swung,
    Till the stars grew pale in the eastern sky.

These were his thoughts, and they pleased him well,
    For his face was lit by a boyish smile.
Urged by an impulse she scarce could tell,
    The nurse stood watching his face the while.

His eyes were bright, but his cheeks were blenched,
    His fevered forehead was hot and damp,
And his long, lean fingers unclenched and clenched,
    And fluttered like moths in the light of the lamp.

Then he turned on his pillow, and crooned a verse
    Of an old bush ballad, uncouth and strange;
She bent above him—his English nurse—
    But the stockman had ridden across the range.

The Hills of Whroo

Oh, the early sun shone brightly
    O'er the ranges green and wide,
And our hearts were beating lightly
    As we cantered side by side,
Down the old bush track together,
    Bidding home and friends adieu,
Faring forth to seek our fortunes
    O'er the bush-clad hills of Whroo.

Overhead, in merry chorus,
    Sang the wild-birds, soft and sweet,
Life's bright pathway stretched before us,
    And our steeds were strong and fleet.
At the bend we paused a moment,
    Ere our old home passed from view,
Then we turned, and cantered gaily
    O'er the bush-clad hills of Whroo.

Through the ironbark and messmate
    Gleamed the wattle, golden-fair,
And the morning winds were laden
    With its fragrance sweet and rare.
Never shadow crossed our pathway,
    Never cloud obscured the blue,
On the morn we went together
    Riding o'er the hills of Whroo.

From our pipes the smoke was curling,
    As, with bridles hanging slack,
At a merry pace we cantered
    Down the winding mountain track.
There was joy in ev'ry motion,
    Strength in ev'ry breath we drew,
On the morn we went a-riding,
    Riding o'er the hills of Whroo.

For the skies were full of sunshine,
    And the bush was blithe with song.
Did it matter where we journeyed,
    Since the days were bright and long?
Never forth rode knights together
    With such faith to dare and do,
As did we that merry morning,
    Riding o'er the hills of Whroo.

Far below us in a hollow
    Slumbr'ing in the morning haze,
Lay the quaint, old mining township,
    Relic of the Roaring Days.
Through its empty streets we cantered,
    And our reins we never drew,
For our thoughts were in the future,
    Riding o'er the hills of Whroo.

But the sun climbed high above us,
    So we reined our steeds at last.
'Neath a spreading gum we rested
    Till the midday heat was past.
Then our steeds again we mounted,
    And we took the track anew,
Riding forth to seek Adventure
    O'er the bush-clad hills of Whroo.

Ah, that ride has long since ended!
    Many years have passed between—
Weary years of toil and sorrow;
    But that mem'ry still is green.
Aye; 'tis verdant green, old comrade,
    But—your grave is verdant, too!
And we'll go no more together,
    Riding o'er the hills of Whroo.

A Cry from the City

Oh! the streets of the city to-night
    Are thronged with a hurrying crowd;
All is laughter, and pleasure, and light,
    And the song of the traffic is loud.

But alone on the pavement I stand,
    Half-dreaming, and vaguely depressed,
While pleasure and youth, hand in hand,
    Flit by with a laugh and a jest.

For alien to me are the sights,
    The splendour, the pomp, and display;
I am dazed by the glare of the lights,
    That hold the grim darkness at bay.

And a voice that I cannot resist,
    O'er the clang and the rattle of cars,
Is calling me out to a tryst
    With Nature, the night, and stars.

I have stood by the gum tree's green bole,
    With my cheek to its sweet-scented bark,
And I've heard the night-wind as it stole,
    Like an elf, through the foliage dark.

I have stood by the shore of the lake,
    As the moon rose resplendent and large,
And heard the waves ripple and break
    In silver-voiced glee on the marge.

I have heard the tall pine, like a harp,
    In the moonlight make melody quaint,
Now singing, insistent and sharp,
    Now murmuring feeble and faint.

I have heard, wafted down from the sky,
    A weird and a mystical croon,
And seen the black swans flitting by,
    Like wraiths, 'twixt the earth and the moon.

Oh! far from the glare and the din,
    From the tramp and the shuffle of feet,
There are pleasures untinctured with sin,
    There are scenes inexpressibly sweet.

Your joys, they are counterfeit joys,
    Your pleasures are mingled with pain,
They are sweet with a sweetness that cloys,
    And they weary the heart and the brain.

But the bush, it is fragrant and fresh,
    Its pleasures are primal and clean,
And the spirit entwined in its mesh
    Recoils from the sordid and mean.

But the heart of the city beats loud,
    Like the throb of a wearisome drum;
I stand 'midst the hurrying crowd,
    And my brain and my bosom are numb.

For, over the roar and the rush,
    Rings a summons insistent and clear,
And my heart has gone forth to the bush,
    And left me disconsolate here.

The Birds

I am the Eagle, emperor of the air,
 No other bird can higher soar than I,
Oft when the cornfields, in the midday glare,
 Are slumbering, you will mark my form on high,
Merging at times into the deep blue sky;
 I am a bird of prey, and, mute with fear,
The Tits and Sparrows, panic-stricken, fly
 Whene'er they see my shadow hovering near.

I am the Crow, the blackest of all birds,
 The blackest, aye, also the wickedest;
I love to hover o'er the dying herds,
 When all the land is bare and drought-distressed.
'Tis then that I enjoy myself the best,
 I have no qualms of conscience, no, nor shame,
Upon the dying beast I come to rest,
 Synonymous with evil is my name.

I am the Magpie, strong of beak and wing,
 Even the Hawk dare not dispute my sway,
For my shrill clarion instantly will bring
 A host of comrades, eager for the fray;
Swiftly we drive the hated foe away,
 My unfledged young I dauntlessly defend;
My voice is first to greet the rising day,
 I am, I am, the farmer's feathered friend.

I am the Jackass, most sedate and wise,
    Gifted by nature with a solemn mien;
No snake or lizard e'er escapes my eyes,
    My sight is so exceptionally keen.
Oft in the Autumn days I can be seen
    In meadows where the ploughman drives his plough,
Hopping the furrows, newly-turned, between,
    And loud I laugh at sunset from the bough.

I am the Ibis, and I love to wade
    Unseen in some secluded woodland pool,
Where lofty gum trees throw their ample shade,
    And ev'rything is undisturbed and cool.
The haunts of man avoiding, as a rule,
    But when the caterpillar doth infest
The fields, and on the farm levy toll,
    I move abroad, and rid him of the pest.

I am the Swan, the poet's fav'rite bird,
    I love to float upon the lake's still breast,
And oft at twilight can my voice be heard,
    When all my kindred have retired to rest,
Flying into the slowly-waning west;
    I love the silence and the solitude
Of reed-fringed lake, wherein to build my nest,
    And, unmolested, rear my quiet brood.

I am the Bittern, and I love the marsh,

    The quiet marsh, wherein to dream and drowse;

My voice is unmelodious and harsh,

    And loud I scream should aught my anger rouse.

My fav'rite haunt is 'neath the trailing boughs,

    Upon the swamps' inhabitants I feed;

A plume of snowy whiteness decks my brows,

    The quiet marsh supplies my ev'ry need,

I am the Spur-winged Plover, sentinel

    And watchful warden of lagoon and lake,

My loud alarum, like a warning bell,

    By day and night the clam'rous echoes wake,

Warning the denizens of bush and brake

    To covert seek, from danger hovering nigh,

My nest in some secluded spot I make,

    And rear my timid young ones, wild and shy.

I am the Skylark, you have heard me oft,

    When the green corn is bursting into ear,

Soaring above the pleasant fields aloft,

    My voice is sweet, melodious, and clear.

The warm September days to me are dear,

    I tarry not when Spring begins to wane,

But move around with the revolving year,

    Following Springtime over land and main.

I am the Swallow, and I come with Spring,
   When op'ning buds their vernal charms display;
Under the eaves I love to climb and cling,
   And in the porch I hang my home of clay.
Toiling and twitt'ring all the livelong day,
   And when my young are fledged—a merry band—
We bid our home adieu, and flit away
   To herald Summer in some distant land.

I am the Sparrow, widely known to all,
   I mind the flutt'ring scarecrow not a whit
In orchard or in cornfield; I am small,
   But somewhat larger than my friend the Tit,
Who, by the by, I can afford to twit,
   Possessing, as I do, a pedigree;
My name is mentioned in the Holy Writ,
   Of which I am as proud as proud can be.

I am the Night Owl, and I sleep all day
   In some secluded corner, out of sight;
But, when the sun has sunk, in search of prey
   I flit abroad, a hunter of the night.
My swift wings make no music in their flight,
   The mice and bats provide my midnight feast,
Anon I whoop, and hide myself away,
   Ere the pale dawn comes creeping in the East.

The Cripple's New Year's Eve

I sit alone by my windowsill,
    My head on my hands (I'm a cripple, you know),
And I watch, as the sun sinks over the hill,
    Bathing the meadows in purple glow.
    The wee birds twitter, the wind breathes low;
All is thoughtful, and sad, and still,
    The year is going where old years go.

To-morrow the sun will rise again
    On a year brought forth from the night's dark womb,
The sad old year, with its toil and pain,
    Will be laid to rest in the silent tomb.
    Fresh hopes will flourish, fresh flowers will bloom.
(The sun sinks lower, the red beams wane,
    The shadowy pinions of darkness loom.)

How strange are the fancies that sickness weaves,
    Or is it fancy? I seem to hear
In the wind that murmurs, and moans, and grieves,
    The feeble breath of the dying year.
    Fainter, fainter, upon my ear,
Mingles the rustle of ivy leaves,
    As the shadowy Angel of Death draws near.

The sun has vanished, the west grows grey,
    The fields are lost in the twilight shade,
The old year dies with the dying day,
    His hours are numbered, his grave is made.
    Oh! Merciful Father! if I have paid
The measure of pain, thou hast bade me pay,
    As the year is fading, so let me fade.

Boundary Bend

It is built of bush timber rough-hewn by the saw;
It is miles from a township and miles from the law;
Its broken-down fence is half-hidden in weeds
And the rubbish that's left when the water recedes
From the posts where the riders once tethered their steeds.
'Tis a tumble-down relic of days that are gone
In a bend where the Murray flows peacefully on,
A favourite haunt of the heron and swan;
'Tis a lonely, old place when the shadows descend
And hide that old shanty at Boundary Bend.

Now it dozes and dreams in the shadows alone
Of the things it has seen in the years that have flown,
What tales it could tell if its walls had a tongue
Of the days long ago when the country was young,
Of the jokes that were played and the songs that were sung
When the bushmen assembled from near and from far,
(The bushmen that *were*—not the bushmen that are!)
To knock down their cheques in the tumble-down bar;
Till, broken and thirsty, their way they would wend
From that crazy, old shanty at Boundary Bend.

On a flat close at hand, where the timber was felled,
On the banks of the river, the races were held.
Ah; that was the glorious day of the year!
And lashin's of liquor and oceans of beer

Were brought to the shanty when race-day drew near;
And the stockmen and drovers and shearers and cooks,
And a pretty fair sprinkling of sharpers and crooks,
Would assemble to battle and bet with the books;
And, sometimes, a squatter or two would attend
That annual meeting at Boundary Bend.

The flag would be lowered, away they would dash,
For riders and horses were reckless and rash;
They would go for their lives from the sound of the gong,
And the fences they raced at were solid and strong;
As with oaths and with curses they thundered along,
Of life and limb they took little account.
And woe to the rider who fell from his mount!
He was lucky indeed if he lived to recount
How he fell when the steeple was nearing its end
At the annual meeting at Boundary Bend.

A bushman in moleskins and tattered, old felt,
With a long, ginger beard sweeping down to his belt,
Presided as judge on an empty gin-case
From a mound where with luck he could view half the race
And roar out the winner in thundering bass;
Then an owner or trainer would tip him a wink
And off he would go to the bar for a drink,
And the liquor would flow and the glasses would clink.
There were thirsts to be quenched, there was money to spend
At the annual meeting at Boundary Bend.

So the meeting went on with its bets and its brawls,
Its rows and its ructions, its protests and falls,
Till the shadows grew lengthy and evening drew near,
And what with libations of whisky and beer,
The judge's decisions grew frightfully queer.
But he cared not a jot how they hooted or cursed,
Once given, his verdict was never reversed!
And he went on contentedly slaking his thirst
Till the crowd got annoyed, and the meeting would end
In an all-around shindy at Boundary Bend.

Now the racecourse is closed and its fences decayed,
And the men of the bush have grown sober and staid;
And the lonely, old shanty stands silent and cold,
And mourns for the men who lie under the mould,
The hard-riding, hard-drinking bushmen of old.
Oh; green be the grass where those riders are laid!
Strong hands and brave hearts of a vanished decade.
They played out the game as the game should be played,
And, maybe, they gather, when shadows descend
In that lonely, old shanty at Boundary Bend.

Thirty-Five

To-night above the windy clouds I watched the sunset die,
And in the silence overhead I heard the swans go by.
The distant hills grew faint and dim and faded from my view,
And darkness fell upon the land and on my spirits too;
A vague regret for something missed: no matter how I strive,
I cannot shake that feeling off. To-day, I'm thirty-five.

Just half of life's allotted span. What solemn thoughts it
    brings!
It's time a fellow looked around and took a stock of things:
To note the credit and the loss, and try to bring to mind
How much of evil and of good the years have left behind.
Of all the golden dreams of youth but very few survive
The jolting on the road of life that leads to thirty-five.

As one who climbs a mountain track looks backward to
    survey
The toilsome path that he has trod upon his upward way,
He sees the whole scene stretched below: far off, he may
    discern
The mountain pathway winding down through tangled
    scrub and fern;
So I have reached a vantage point from which I may derive
A clear perspective of the road that led to thirty-five.

Ah me; it is a winding road, the road whereon I've strayed!
I see the false turns that I took, the blunders that I made.
The easy road that lured me on until I woke to find
The path that led to happiness was one I'd left behind.
But taking matters all in all I'm lucky to arrive
Safe at the half-way house of life, the age of thirty-five.

I might have married years ago; I should have done in fact.
I loved the girl and she loved me: 'twas courage that I lacked.
That sad night haunts my mem'ry still, the night when last we kissed.
I bitterly regret at times the happiness I missed;
But all that now is past and done: 'tis useless to revive
The tender dreams of twenty-one when we are thirty-five.

The war cut out a slice of life, and yet I'm bound to say
I would re-live it all again had I the chance to-day.
The bonds of comradeship were strong that bound us each to each.
In war's grim school are lessons learned that nothing else can teach.
The bitter scenes are fading fast, the brighter ones survive;
It's pleasant to recall them now when I am thirty-five.

I used to dream long years ago about a perfect state,
A place where there would be no poor or any rich or great,
Where all would be on equal terms; but I have found since
> then
No legislation can ensure the happiness of men.
You'll find black sheep in every flock and drones in ev'ry hive,
We've very few illusions left when we are thirty-five.

The wondrous progress man has made the last two thousand
> years
Has done but little to reduce his sum of doubts and fears.
The powers of air and earth and sea are harnessed to his will
And yet the goal of his desires eludes and mocks him still.
We cannot compass all our dreams no matter how we strive;
You learn to take things as they come when you are
> thirty-five.

Ah well! a truce to bitter thoughts. The moon is rising now,
The ev'ning winds begin to lay soft fingers on my brow.
The Bird of Time, as Omar says, is always on the wing.
You never know what happiness to-morrow's dawn may
> bring!
And after all is said and done it's *good* to be alive;
We've much to live and hope for yet though we are
> thirty-five!

The Ballad of Mick O'Bree

In Joe Dunn's shanty one New Year's Eve we were drinking and swopping lies,
When Mick O'Bree on his wall-eyed mare came cantering over the rise;
The wall-eyed mare that he always rode and nobody else could ride,
He jumped to the ground by the shanty door and tethered the mare outside.

He asked the boys if they'd have a drink, and of course they said they would,
But Dunn looked out at the wall-eyed mare, and asked if the bet still stood.
And Mick replied as he raised his glass in a voice that was rather dry:
"Well, there's the mare by the fence out there if anyone wants to try.

Ev'ryone of you know the bet, and I think that the bet is fair;
I'll give a fiver to any man who can ride the wall-eyed mare.
But if they don't, and I know they won't, they must make for the nearest bar,
And buy her owner, Mick O'Bree, a bottle of best 'Three Star'."

"Oh yes, the wager is fair enough," said Dunn in his quiet way,
"But this sultry weather has knocked me up and I won't have a go to-day.
I have no doubt I could ride her out—just look at her standing there!
But I'd rather waltz with a wall-eyed girl than ride on your wall-eyed mare!"

O'Bree was a bushman born and reared, of the decent carefree sort,
He liked a drink and he liked a joke, and was always out for sport.
He never said how the mare was bred or the price he had paid for her,
We only knew that he rode her hard and tamed her with whip and spur.

The wind had blown from the North all day and the bar was rather warm,
And Dunn remarked as he mopped his brow we were in for a thunderstorm;
But no one worried about the heat while the talk and the drinks flowed free,
And ev'ryone laughed at the lies of Dunn and the tales of Mick O'Bree.

Night came down, and we heard the roll of the thunder far away,
The skies were sullen and inky black, and we pressed O'Bree to stay.
But Mick was now in a reckless mood and he said as he drained his glass:
"Some other fellow may pinch my girl if I wait for the storm to pass.
There's a dance you know in the town to-night and whether it's foul or fair,
A girl will wait by her garden gate for O'Bree and his wall-eyed mare.
So fill your glasses for one last drink and then we will all shake hands,
And don't forget to remind your mates that O'Bree and his bet still stands.
That wall-eyed mare that you joke about and you're all too scared to ride,
There's not another to match with her from here to the Lachlan side!
A little peevish at times maybe but safe as a lady's hack,
If I wanted to gallop to Hell to-night she would carry me there and back!"

He mounted close to the shanty door and the bay mare tossed her head,
As he swung to his seat with the easy grace of a horseman born and bred.
She bounded straight for the open road and we shouted a last farewell,
As a flash of lightning cleft the sky and the first big raindrop fell.

And then it came with the pent-up wrath of a storm that is long delayed,
And most of us thought of our sinful souls as the shanty rocked and swayed.
The rafters groaned and the hail bounced in through the door that was half ajar,
And the bottles rattled upon the shelf and the glasses on the bar.

Quicker and quicker the lightning flashed and louder the thunder pealed,
And the tempest tore at the roof and walls till we thought they would have to yield.
But I heard Dunn bellow above the din, "Was there ever a storm like this?
God help O'Bree on that wall-eyed mare if anything goes amiss!"

The thunder rolled away to the North and the wind died
    down at last,
The rain still beat on the shanty roof but the worst of the
    storm was past,
When drenched to the skin a man reeled in, white-faced,
    through the open door.
He swayed a moment then dumped his swag with a gasp on
    the bar-room floor.

He pointed out to the night and cried, and his voice was
    hoarse and weak:—
"There's a dead man lying beside the road back there by the
    Wonga Creek!
As God's my judge I'm telling the truth, though none of you
    here know me;
I saw his face when the lightning flashed, it's my brother,
    Mick O'Bree!"

We harnessed a buggy; we raced away while the lightning
    round us played,
And Dunn kept cursing the wall-eyed mare as the old trap
    rocked and swayed.
"She was only waiting her chance," he said, "from the day
    that he broke her in,
He laughed when I called her the wall-eyed witch, but I
    knew that the witch would win!"

We were somewhere close to the Wonga Creek when a flicker of lightning showed
A huddled figure beneath a tree by the side of the rain-washed road.
And then I knew Dunn's words were true; she had gripped the bit in her teeth,
And dashed his head on a leaning limb as she shot like a bolt beneath.

We lifted him up but we saw at once there was nothing that we could do,
For the top of his forehead was all crushed in and his neck was broken too,
And there by the light of a smoky lamp and the lightning's baleful glare,
We had a look at the handiwork of the vicious wall-eyed mare.

We started back on our lonely drive and Dunn kept saying to me,
"I hope the whisky has done its work on that brother of Mick O'Bree.
If Kelly has carried my orders out and got him away to bed,
I'll wipe his tally right off the slate; he can shout for the boys instead."

I didn't answer, I only thought that it looked like the hand of Fate:—
A waiting woman, a wall-eyed mare, and a brother who came too late.
We carried him into the bar that night, and we sat and we waked him there,
And that is the story of Mick O'Bree, and the wicked wall-eyed mare.

Shylock Revised

There were queer old laws in Venice if Bill Shakespeare's tale
    is true,
Of the way they dealt with Shylock when his pound of flesh
    fell due.
I maintain the law was rotten, and the judge's verdict wrong,
And the critics and the actors have misled us all along.
Ev'ry time I read the story, I can feel my doubts increase
That the Bard intended Shylock as the villain of the piece.
But of course so many actors would not want to play the part
If a pound of flesh was skewered from a region near their
    heart.
And it might be an advantage if the play had ended so,
It would rid the boards forever of some actors that I know!
But looking at the matter in a quite impartial way,
I am sure that poor old Shylock is the hero of the play.

You must study Shylock deeply if you'd understand the case,
And to note he had the vices and the virtues of his race.
He was shrewd and keen in business, cold and resolute and
    proud,
While the men he had to deal with were a drunken wastrel
    crowd.
From the lower form of vices, he was totally exempt,
But the bold Venetians were *not*, and he held them in
    contempt.

They were jealous of his fortune, and they pried in his affairs,
But they got almighty savage if he interfered in theirs.
They would borrow money from him when their funds were getting slack,
Then abuse him and revile him when he came and asked it back.
They were grand old types of Christians lived in Venice long ago—
They were very near the equal of some modern ones I know!

So they baited him and mocked him in their kindly Christian way,
But he stood it all with patience like a grand old stag at bay.
See him on the old Rialto with his long white flowing beard,
And Antonio spitting at him while the crowd stood by and jeered!
Mean and cowardly and cruel as the rabble always are,
Though old Shylock was the nobler and the better man by far!
But his only shield was silence; there was none to take his part,
Though it might have stirred some pity in the hardest Christian heart.

Shylock had an only daughter and he thought the world of her;
He'd no one else to care for—he'd been left a widower.
But she bolted with Lorenzo, just a rake around the town,
And she pinched his jewels and ducats and she took the old man down.

Goaded almost past endurance can we wonder at his grief,
When he found his only daughter was a low down common thief.
Then to cap it all Antonio borrowed money for his friend,
And could not repay the ducats when three months were at an end.
And old Shylock feeling bitter when he had him in the mesh,
Swore a mighty oath to Heaven he would have his pound of flesh.

And I believe he would have got it if he'd had a decent judge—
One who would have probed the reason for the old man's bitter grudge.
But unluckily for Shylock, e'er the trial had well began,
Portia came post haste from Belmont masquerading as a man.
She had eloquence and beauty and her entrance caused a stir,
And the Duke straightway decided he would leave the case to her.

From the point of view of justice 'twas a fatal interlude,
For her arguments were biased and illogical and crude.
She had come to save the merchant from the wronged and wrathful Jew,
And her woman's wit was equal to the task she'd come to do.
For she twisted him and turned him and enmeshed him in the law,
And she got the old man flustered when she touched him on the raw.

Shylock! Shylock! Poor old Shylock! I can sympathize with
    you!
Had I been in your position I'd have claimed the forfeit due,
And the quality of mercy, of which Portia seemed so fond,
I'd have flung to far Gehenna; *I'd have stood upon my bond!*

But the judgment went against him as old Shylock might
    have known,
With a crowd like that to deal with, and he left the court
    alone.
Pale, dispirited and broken, mute with grief, and choked
    with rage,
Surely the most tragic figure that has ever trod the stage!

Shylock! Shylock! Poor old Shylock! 'Twas a bitter cup to quaff,
When you heard Antonio pleading with the Duke to let you
    off.
He, the serpent that had stung you, 'twas indeed a bitter
    draught,
So you left the court in silence while the whole crowd jeered
    and laughed.
Half your wealth forfeit to Venice, but I'm quite prepared to
    say,
That you had it back with interest ere a year had passed away!
And the very crowd that mocked you when they got you on
    your own,
Sympathized and sided with you ere they touched you for a
    loan;

For, despite their Christian conscience, what with girls, and
    cards, and booze,
You were just the institution they could not afford to lose!
Anyhow, I hope you prospered till, content and crowned
    with years,
You went down amongst your fathers from this vale of grief
    and tears.

And Portia, sleek-faced Portia, with her knowledge of the law,
I will guarantee Bassanio soon got tired of her jaw!
Though her afterlife's not mentioned by the late lamented
    Bard,
I have always had a notion that her married lot was hard.
That her sons, if she had any, went completely to the bad,
And her daughters married wasters—fortune hunters like
    their Dad;
That Bassanio boozed her money, and then made a final dash
Out of Belmont with a barmaid and the remnants of her cash.
And I'm sure that she discovered when they brought the
    bailiffs in,
And she sued for some assistance to her kindly Christian kin,
That the homily on mercy she delivered to the Jew,
Was required pretty badly by some Christian bosoms too.
Leave her to her sad reflections—if she hadn't butted in,
I am sure that poor old Shylock would have got a better spin.

And the old man's strumpet daughter, who can waste a
   thought on her?
Since she bit the hand that fed her like a mean, ungrateful cur.
It is bootless to conjecture how she fared in later life,
But we know she robbed her father and became Lorenzo's
   wife.
I suppose he pawned her trinkets and her wedding ring to
   boot,
And went bolting out of Venice with the bailiffs in pursuit.
'Tis a likely supposition, and it served her right because
From the first she knew quite clearly what a useless cad he
   was.
And I have a shrewd suspicion, nay, I'm pretty sure indeed,
She went crawling back to Shylock for forgiveness and a feed;
And he probably forgave her, being broken and unnerved,
But he should have sent her packing; it was what the minx
   deserved!

Shylock! Shylock! Poor old Shylock! I can sympathize with
   you.
I've been in the hands of villains; I've been robbed and
   baited too.
You were scandalously treated, and I will not rest content,
Till I re-arrange your story in the way that Shakespeare
   meant.
And I'll see that you get justice when I try the case afresh;
Portia will not be admitted—*you will get your pound of flesh!*

A Little Bit of Land

I've been working in the city, but I've turned my billet in,
For my nerves are worn to fragments with the bustle and the din.
It's a hand-to-mouth existence, just a ceaseless, dull routine,
And a man is but a robot, just a cog in the machine.
So I'm leaving it forever, and I've got my future planned,
For at last I am the owner of a little bit of land.

I was reared 'way up the country but I left it long ago,
For the thoughts of city pleasures set my youthful heart aglow.
But I found like many others that its joys were mostly sham,
That its gold was dross and tinsel, and its jobs not worth a damn.
Now, henceforward and forever, all the diamonds on the Rand
Would not lure me to the city from my little bit of land.

When you reach the age of thirty and you want to settle down
You will find there's little prospect in the selfish, sordid town.
You will soon be on your uppers if you chance to lose your job,
And the world is hard and callous when you haven't got a bob.
But you've always got an asset and some credit at command
When you hold the deeds and title to a little bit of land.

For old Adam took to farming, as the Bible bids us b'lieve,
When he got the sack from Eden through the cussedness of Eve.
I've no doubt he growled a little when he had to yoke the plough
Or discovered after sundown that he had to milk the cow,
But I'll bet that they were happy as they wandered hand in hand
Round the waving corn in springtime on their little bit of land.

You will get no further forward while you're working for a boss,
And he'll tramp you mighty sudden when he starts to show a loss,
And you'll just keep drifting, drifting in an aimless sort of way,
Kicked about from post to pillar, living just from day to day.
But you've got a solid anchor, and the liberty is grand,
That is yours when you're the owner of a little bit of land.

You have something then to live for; you can call your soul your own,
And you'll have your share of leisure when your land is ploughed and sown.
You can talk of sheep and cattle, and the price of wool and grain;
You're a partner in the seasons, in the sunshine and the rain,
And I think that God intended when this universe He planned
That we all should be the owners of a little bit of land.

A Cry from the Mallee

I'm sitting alone in the Mallee scrub watching the sun go
 down,
Long miles away from the nearest pub, and miles from the
 nearest town,
The wind has eddied and swirled all day, but now it has sunk
 to rest,
And I feel fed-up as I gaze away at the sombre, silent west.

They settled us here when the war was won, in a region of
 scrub and sand,
The reward for a duty nobly done, the gift of a grateful land.
We toiled like niggers to clear our blocks, we slaved in the
 dust and heat
Lured on by the vision of thriving flocks and paddocks of
 waving wheat.

And this is the harvest of all our hopes, the fruits of our
 simple trust:
A stretch of barren and wind-swept slopes that redden the
 skies with dust;
And this is the measure of all we've won from seasons of
 ceaseless work—
I'd sooner be fighting the Christian Hun or chasing the
 pagan Turk!

Remote and distant and out of reach are the pleasure of
  Auld Lang Syne;
Oh! for a stroll on the breezy beach, or a plunge in the
  cooling brine;
No wonder a man gets down in the dumps with sand in his
  hair and boots,
When he isn't grubbing the flaming stumps he's cutting the
  Mallee shoots!

But, sooner or later, the drought must break, and the seasons
  change again,
We still have faith though our hearts may ache—and we'll
  battle along till then.
You'll get most things if you're game to fight, and we'll reap
  our just reward
When fortune smiles and the sun shines bright on hope—
  and a land restored!

Pulling Teats

I was reared on a selection; I'm a product of the land,
For my old man had a dairy and we milked the cows by hand.
I can still recall the cow-yard and the cow-shed roofed with bark,
Where we rounded up the cattle, and we milked them in the dark.
And they used to take some finding in the dawnlight cold and bleak,
For they'd hide among the timber in the paddock by the creek.
But we somehow always found them scattered here, and scattered there,
And we'd send them flying homeward with old Rover in the rear.
They would scamper to the cow-yard where they'd stand and chew the cud
Till we waded out to milk them in the slush and in the mud.
Oh, my youth was sadly blighted, and my young dreams went to bits
While those precious hours I wasted in the cow-shed pulling teats!

They were sulky, stubborn beggars, but of all the cows we had
There was none to try the patience of a silent, suffering lad
Like the bald-faced brindle heifer that we bought at Riley's sale;
For your woes were only starting when you got her in the bail.
She was obstinate and crafty, and her teats were sore to boot,
And we used to fight like blazes over who would milk the brute.
When you slipped the leg-rope on her, if you were not mighty quick
She would land you in the mullock with a well-directed kick.
Then you'd lamb her with the leg-rope or you'd whack her with the stool,
But she didn't take much notice; she was stubborn as a mule.
She would bide her time in patience till she got you off your guard,
Then she'd swing her mud-caked tail-piece, and she'd catch you good and hard.
Oh, the tricks she played upon us nearly drove us into fits,
So we sold her to the butcher, and we reckoned we were quits.

When our old man had his breakfast he would mooch about the shed,
But he never took on milking, he had never learned, he *said*;
And we had a shrewd suspicion that he never meant to try!
But *we* had to do our duty 'neath the stern, paternal eye.
He was good at giving orders, and he made us milk 'em dry!
For he came from Tipperary where they don't do things by halves,
And we had to wash the buckets and we had to feed the calves.
Then we'd gobble down our breakfast and set off with books and slate
To the schoolhouse at the Crossing, and get whacked for being late;
Where the master, honest fellow, laboured hard throughout the day
To impart his knowledge to us, but our brains were all astray,
And his misdirected efforts turned him prematurely grey,
For he never seemed to notice that our sadly muddled wits
Couldn't rise above the cow-yard and the job of pulling teats!

Now, I've bade goodbye for ever to the cold and slushy yard
Where my youthful life was blighted, and my youthful dreams were marred.
I am living in the city, and I rarely see a cow,
But the thoughts of Riley's heifer set my blood a-boiling now;
And when'er I read the verses of some sentimental bard
Singing of the joys of farming, I am always on my guard.
If I ever chance to meet him, I have registered a vow
If he dares to use his talent to apostrophise the cow,
I'll place something more than laurels on his corrugated brow!
And I warn all future parents if they'd save their kids from harm,
For the love of Mike don't bring them within *cooee* of a farm!
For I lost my fond illusions, and my young dreams went to bits
When those precious hours I wasted in the cow-yard pulling teats!

On the Rail of the Bar

When you've finished your job in the country
    And you're due for a bit of a rest,
You will pack up your things in a hurry,
    And rig yourself out in your best.
You will purchase a brief to the city
    With fifty or so on your hip;
You'll be feeling as fit as a fiddle
    Like a sailor just off from his ship;
You will drift to a snug little bar-room
    And order a glass of "Three Star",
With your elbow at rest on the counter,
    And your foot on the rail of the bar.

And someone will come and accost you,
    And greet you as Harry or Jack,
And say that he knew you in boyhood,
    Or shore with you somewhere Out Back.
And some of his mates will be with him,
    (There are always a couple or more),
And you'll soon be like brothers together
    Though you may not have met them before.
But your mind will be calm and contented;
    Your joy there'll be nothing to mar,
With your elbow at rest on the counter,
    And your foot on the rail of the bar.

Though you may hate the saltbush like poison,
    And have sworn you will never go back,
Your language will grow quite poetic
    As you speak of the joys of the track.
They will listen in mute admiration
    To your tales of the river and run,
Of the deeds you have done in the saddle,
    Or the races you've ridden and won,
Of the mates you have fenced with and shorn with,
    And camped with and tramped with afar—
With your elbow at rest on the counter,
    And your foot on the rail of the bar.

You will tell how you rode for the doctor,
    And forded the Darling in flood,
And landed at dawn at the township,
    Half-naked and covered in mud;
How you rode the worst horse on the station
    Till you had him as quiet as a mouse.
Then the landlord will rap on the counter
    And say there are drinks on the house.
And someone will call for a soda,
    And someone will have a cigar,
And you'll say he's a jolly good fellow,
    With your foot on the rail of the bar.

And your language will grow more expansive
    As the brandy's beginning to work,
And you'll take them away out to glory
    To a station far westward of Bourke,
Where you ran down the red-coated dingo,
    The terror of Willoughby's Soak,
And rode to the Seven Creeks' muster
    On a horse that was barely half-broke,
And your jacket was ripped into ribbons
    As you raced through the scrub and belar—
With your elbow at rest on the counter,
    And your foot on the rail of the bar.

When everyone's talking together
    And everyone's eager to shout,
You will twist for awhile off the brandy
    And order a beer or a stout.
Then you'll tell how you landed one Christmas
    Stone-broken at Boundary Bend,
And met by the best of good fortune
    A mate with a tenner to spend,
And you got into holts with a shearer,
    A fellow who thought he could spar,
But you hit him a beaut on the boko
    And knocked him clean out of the bar.

So the spree will go merrily onward
>   Till you've tried half the drinks on the shelf,
And you've told all the lies you can think of
>   Till you almost believe them yourself;
Till your tongue gets a little bit tangled
>   And your brain isn't feeling too clear,
And you think it's the heat of the bar-room
>   That is making your stomach so queer.
Then you'll tell them to fill up their glasses
>   No matter how many there are,
And, feeling a trifle unsteady,
>   You will toddle away from the bar.

When you're way back again in the country,
>   And lying stone-broke in your tent,
And the curlews are calling around you,
>   You will mourn for the money you spent.
When the scenes of the past are receding
>   In a vapour of brandy and beer,
You will mentally swear to keep sober
>   When you visit the city next year.
But, drifting away into slumber,
>   When the doorway of dreams is ajar,
You will think you are back in the city
>   With your foot on the rail of the bar.

Lightning

There's lightning away in the West to-night, away where the
    sun went down,
But I stand alone in the glare and light in the heart of the
    noisy town.
The pavement echoes with laugh and jest as the theatre
    crowds flit by,
But my heart is filled with a vague unrest as I gaze at the
    stormy sky.

For I was born in the great Out Back, and my heart it is still
    out there
Where the clouds are gathering inky black, and the
    lightnings flame and flare;
Where the drover waits while the thunders crash and the
    threatening tempest nears,
To the frightened bellow and maddened dash of the wild,
    stampeding steers.

Away out there where the ranges dip to plains that are wide and green,
There are honest hands that a man may grip, and know that the hands are clean.
They know the meaning of Mateship there, and their word is their only bond,
Where thunders mutter and lightnings flare out there in the Great Beyond.

Oh, the streets of the city are bright and warm,
And the careless crowd goes by;
It's little they care for the stress and storm far out where the ranges lie.
But my heart is filled with a vague unrest, and I feel like a renegade
As I gaze away at the stormy west where the lightnings flame and fade.

The Old Blade Shed

'Twas a calm, clear eve in the late November,
    And the hills were flushed with the sunset red
When I reined my horse in the clump of timber
    To gaze again on the old blade shed.
A hush of sorrow, an air of mourning
    Brooded over the quiet scene,
But a plover uttered a cry of warning,
    And an ibis rose from the reed-beds green.

For thirty years had the sunsets mellowed
    On its roof of tin, and its walls of wood;
The rains had beaten, and winds had bellowed,
    But strong and sturdy the old shed stood.
The bush around it had changed to meadows,
    And the wheat waved high where the sheep had fed,
But the gums still whispered, and threw their shadows
    Night and morn on the old blade shed.

There is always something of sadness after
    In viewing the scenes of our early years,
The spot that rang to our childish laughter
    Or saw the fall of our foolish tears.
I gazed again on the well-known places
    And memory gathered each broken thread,
And I heard the voices and saw the faces
    Of the men who shore in the old blade shed.

And my mind went back to the years departed,

    To the warm spring days when the pens were full,
When the bell was rung and the shearers started,

    And their blades bit deep in the soft, white wool.
And, again, in fancy I saw them bending

    With beaded brows while their breaths came deep,
And I heard the click of the shearblades blending

    With the yell for tar and the bleat of sheep.

I was only a lad, but I loved to linger

    And watch and listen, all eyes and ears.
From the rouseabout to the bearded ringer

    I knew them all in those far-off years.
And they told me tales of the runs far distant,

    Of the sprees they had, and the lives they led,
And my heart beat fast as I sat and listened

    Years ago in the old blade shed.

Now gone forever the old-time glories,

    The bleat of sheep and the click of shears.
Hushed and ended the wondrous stories

    That rang so sweet in my boyish ears.
I always wanted to be a rover,

    The sky my roof, and the earth my bed,
But long ere the days of my youth were over,

    I bade goodbye to the old blade shed.

The evening shadows were falling round me
    When I sighed and woke from my dream at last,
For broken now were the bonds that bound me
    To this quiet scene in the years long past.
The friends of my boyhood were gone forever
    And the dreams that gladdened my youth were dead,
And I turned my horse with a sudden shiver
    And rode away from the old blade shed.

Not To-day

By George; I must have been drunk last night—
    I have such an awful head!
And I quite forgot to put out the light
    Before I got into bed.
'Tis years and years since I've been so full,
    The party was pretty gay.
I must give up parties and take a pull,
    But I must have a drink to-day.

A man's a fool when he comes to think!
    For years I have toiled and slaved,
But what with races, and cards and drink
    I haven't a penny saved.
A chap should open a bank account
    And add to it ev'ry pay.
Next week I'll start with a small amount
    But I haven't the cash to-day.

I borrowed a tenner from poor old Joe
    At the races when last we met.
It must be nearly a year ago,
    And I haven't repaid him yet.
He'll think a fellow's forgotten it quite,
    Or he doesn't intend to pay.
I must send him a tenner when next I write,
    But I haven't the time to-day.

'Tis time that I married and settled down,
    Got hold of a true, young wife.
For years I've been knocking around the town,
    Just wasting away my life.
Peggy is pretty and Rose is sweet,
    But the best of them all is May.
I must pluck up courage when next we meet
    And ask her—but not to-day!

No, not today; oh, you careless elf,
    You'll be always prepared to shun
The things you should do, and excuse yourself
    For the things you have left undone!
When the undertaker calls around for you,
    Then some of your friends will say:—
"Poor beggar; he had such a lot to do—
    But they're burying him to-day!"

Cats on the Roof

The street where I live is a forest of flats,
And it's cursed by a plague of most insolent cats.
As soon as the sun has gone down in the west
They all sally forth on an amorous quest.
A tomcat will call from the top of a roof,
Another will answer from somewhere aloof;
Then others arrive, and the concert begins
As they slither and slide on the tiles and the tins.

Cats on the roof! cats on the roof!
Amorous, clamorous cats on the roof!
White ones and yellow ones; black-as-Othello-ones!
Oh, the devil's in league with the cats on the roof!

We talk of the Japs and the need for defence,
But what we require is someone of sense
To supply us with rifles, machine-guns, and bombs
To use on the tabs and the turbulent toms
Who gather in numbers that nightly increase,
To shatter our slumbers and slaughter our peace.
Oh, he's sure of a title and plenty of oof
Who deals with the menace of cats on the roof!

They climb and they clamber; they hiss, and they wail,
And go up and down on the musical scale.
A shy, young soprano will start on a note
While the ardent old tenor is clearing his throat.
Then off they will go on a dainty duet,
And the bass will come in when the tempo is set;
And any young student of sharps and of flats
Can learn quite a lot from this choir of the cats!

Then, all of a sudden, the tempo will change—
They really possess a most wonderful range,
From alto, contralto, falsetto and bass;
Caruso and Melba are not in the race!
The tenor will rise on a note of his *own*,
And the bass will die off to a horrible moan.
Oh, I doubt if the patience of Job would be proof
Against amorous, clamorous cats on the roof!

A lull may occur when the midnight is past,
And you'll think you are set for some slumber at last,
But just as you're dozing, your face to the wall,
The concert will end in a terrible brawl!
And you'll turn on your pillow and mentally vow
To kill all the cats that you meet with from now.
Then morning comes in with a dusting of mats,
And another night's rest has been ruined by cats.

Cats on the roof! cats on the roof!
Amorous, clamorous cats on the roof!
White ones and yellow ones; black-as-Othello-ones!
Oh, the devil's in league with the cats on the roof!

Retrospect

The sun went down with splendid pomp
    Beyond the mountain wall,
And from the lonely reed-fringed swamp
    The plaintive curlews call.
The secret things that love the night
    Come forth to prey and roam,
And swiftly through the waning light
    The last, lone bird flits home.

The twilight deepens round my hut,
    No shadow moves in sight,
But Lass, my half-bred dingo slut,
    Snarls out upon the night.
Down, girl; the darkness hides no foe;
    No danger hovers near.
'Tis but the reed-beds murm'ring low,
    The night-wind that you hear.

And yet, and yet, I, somehow, feel
    That I am not alone.
Across the night, old voices steal
    From out the vast unknown.
I hear the clink of spur and rein,
    The muffled tramp of steeds;
Above the night-wind's low refrain,
    The murmur of the reeds.

Ah me, those dreams of Sinai,
    Those longings, wild and vain;
Old memories that will not die,
    Old wounds that bleed again!
My mind is filled with vague regret,
    And fancies wild and strange,
(The sunset glory lingers yet
    Above the gloomy range.)

It lingers yet, and, like the beams
    Around the setting sun,
A sombre glory gilds the dreams
    Of days long past and done:
The days of movement, life, and zest,
    When baleful beacons glowed,
And splendid legions marched abreast
    Down Duty's open road.

Memories

Oh, the sands of the desert again are calm, the tempest has
  overblown;
The wind may whisper its age-old psalm over the sandwaste
  lone.
No more at the clatter of steel-clad hoofs do the startled
  children fly,
Or the Arab women forsake their roofs as the brown brigades
  sweep by.

The sun will rise, and the sun will set on minaret, mosque,
  and tomb,
But the desert children will not forget the men of the Emu
  plume,
The long, lean men with the careless laugh who traversed the
  wastes of sand,
And scattered the Moslem foes like chaff wherever they
  sought to stand.

Ah, they were splendid, those days of old! I was younger and
  stronger then,
But I'd barter all that the years may hold to ride in the ranks
  again,
To ride once more down the shell-torn slope to the skyline
  black with hate,
However forlorn might be the hope, with Death as a section
  mate!

But times have altered, and it is vain to grieve for a bygone day,
My mates of the stirrup and spur and rein have passed like a dream away,
They come no more at the bugle call, they are scattered the wide world o'er,
For the bond is broken that bound us all on the bitter fields of war.

The sand drifts over the lonely graves far out on the wastes of Sin,
And the Emu feather no longer waves in Cairo's glare and din ...
But dead or living, or near or far, they will answer no call of mine.
Well, I wish them luck wherever they are for the sake of the Auld Lang Syne!

And our bush-bred horses who stood the test, to hunger and hardship steeled,
They, too, are lying by ridge and crest on many a desert field.
They were true to the country that gave them birth, and I hold their mem'ry dear;
There were hearts as brave 'neath the saddle-girth as under the bandolier!

Mates of the desert, there's little we know, and less that we understand,
But, sooner or later, we all must go on the Last Adventure grand.
Who knows? Mayhap, on that sunset shore, regiment and brigade,
Rider and steed, we may meet once more on one last Great Parade.

Billy Woods

Billy Woods, the night is falling, and I'm lying here alone
In a bend beside the Lachlan, dreaming of the years long flown.
All around the winds are sighing, and a muffled murmur comes,
Like the sound of mocking laughter or the roll of distant drums.

I have tramped all day, old comrade, with the hot wind in my face,
And I felt done-up and beaten when I reached this quiet place,
For old age is creeping on me and my lungs are not too sound,
And at night the coughing wakes me when I'm lying on the ground.

Many years have passed, old comrade, since that far, eventful day
When we watched our shores receding through the darkness and the spray,
As we stood on deck together on the transport, outward bound,
With the wheeling gulls above us and the tumbling seas around.

It was pleasant in the moonlight just to sit and smoke at ease
As our boat went plunging onward o'er the phosphorescent
   seas,
Or to sing a rousing chorus and beguile the hours with song.
Did it matter where we journeyed? We were young, and we
   were strong!

Sometimes now, when all is quiet, and I close my eyes
   awhile,
Once again I see old Cairo by the mem'ry-haunted Nile,
Where our emu-plumes went waving through the tumult
   and the din,
And we took our fill of pleasure and we steeped our souls in
   sin.

But the world was topsy-turvy and we were not all to blame,
And we paid a bitter penance when the call to battle came.
How we cursed those Moslem gunners, far away and out of
   reach,
Ere we bade good-bye for ever to that shell-swept Anzac
   beach!

Back again we came to Egypt, still together, you and I,
And the bush brigades marched northward o'er the sands of
   Sinai.
Out across the hazy ridges where the scorching khamsin blew,
Where, alone, the grit and courage of our horses pulled us
   through.

On the white sands of Romani, in the hush before the dawn,
There was little quarter given when we met with bayonets drawn,
But we hurled them back at sunset, and we drove them o'er
   the sand
Till the mountains rose before us, and we saw the Holy Land.

Back we reeled from shell-torn Gaza when the day was almost
   done,
For the Turkish line was broken, and we had them on the run.
But the heavy night descended over mound, and mosque, and
   tomb,
As we rode, repulsed, and cursing, through the silence and
   the gloom.

Many a night we lay together underneath the starry dome,
And a hush would fall between us as our thoughts went
   wandering home.
Vague regrets and heartsick longings, thoughts too deep for
   words or speech—
But the loneliness and danger bound us closer, each to each.

In a barren rock-strewn wady all day long as we watched and
   cursed,
Standing by our weary horses, caked with sweat and parched
   with thirst.
Stubbornly the Turks were holding; night was near, and
   things looked black,
With the shell-swept ridge before us and the desert at our back.

"*Mount!*" A sharp, staccato order, and the squadrons swung in line
In the last, red glare of sunset, and the lead began to whine.
On the hill we poised a moment, and it seemed a slender hope,
As we spurred our tired horses down that shell-tormented slope.

Every gun was turned upon us, and the sand flew up like spray
As we raced towards the trenches where the foemen stood at bay.
To the left, machine-guns rattled in a deadly enfilade,
But they could not stem the onrush of that reckless bush brigade.

Shrapnel shrieked and mausers rattled, and the bombs came whirling down;
Riders reeled and horses stumbled as the squadrons neared the town.
But we swept across their trenches in a swirl of blood and foam,
And a ringing cheer went skyward as the squadrons thundered home.

Through the blazing town we galloped, and the Moslems broke and fled,
And the shades of night descended on the dying and the dead.

In the dim, grey light we mustered by the shattered railway
    bridge...
Then they told me you were lying out upon that shell-swept
    ridge.

At the break of day I sought you and I found you lying there
With the red blood on your tunic, and the red sand in your
    hair;
Lying just as you had fallen, and I knelt and pressed your
    hand—
Oh! the hopes, the dreams, the longings that lie buried in
    the sand...

Now the war is long since over, and I'm tramping in the
    West,
And I sometimes think, old comrade, after all you fared the
    best.
You are better off than I am in your far-off desert grave,
For a man must tramp for tucker in the land he fought to
    save.

But I'm getting very sleepy and the night will soon be flown,
And the gums are whispering secrets in a muffled undertone.
We may meet again, old comrade, when we hear the final
    call,
And the bush brigades are mustered for the Last Parade of
    all.

If Morgan Knew

Kildare was bidding a long farewell to the heat, the wind, and the sand,
And he bore a letter to Morgan's wife written in Morgan's hand.
We said good-bye, and we wished him luck, and we sighed as we saw him go,
Then turned again to our bitter task with a curse for the Moslem foe.
Hotter and hotter the long days grew, and the Jackos' still held the town.
The monitors roared at the break of day, and they roared when the sun went down.
For the heights of Gaza were hard to take, with its cactus hedge ablaze—
It was boot and saddle from morn till night through the warm September days.
Kildare was forgotten until, somehow, the story filtered through:
He was home and living with Morgan's wife—and we wondered if Morgan knew!

Morgan was always a quiet chap; he never had much to say.
A long, lean bushman, he did his bit in the same old, silent way.
Someone suggested he should be told—it would come to him soon or late—

But the notion didn't appeal to me, for I was his section mate.
Whether the story was true or false, it was simply his own concern...
So the weeks went by, and he seemed to grow a little more taciturn.
A letter came to one of the boys and it seemed that the yarn was true,
But I shut my mouth, for I thought, somehow, there'd be trouble if Morgan knew.

An order came for a move at last, a dash on the Moslem flank,
And we rode from the shadow of Fara mound as the red sun waned and sank.
We marched all night through the Dead Sea waste, and I'll never forget that ride
Through rock-strewn wadis and leagues of sand, with only the stars to guide.
But we reached our goal ere the dawn of day, and, to render them honour due,
It was only the grit of our bush-bred steeds that pulled their riders through.

We halted at last in a bouldered gorge and the thunder of guns grew loud,
And over Beersheba the dust and smoke hung like a sable shroud.
But the Turks were making a stubborn stand, and the sun was almost down

When the squadrons mounted and swung in line on a ridge
    above the town.
It was then the need for a ground scout came to see if the
    path was clear,
To gallop away to the front alone, and they called for a volunteer.
It seemed a gallop to certain death. I was sorry when Morgan
    spoke.
But he rode away with a careless nod through a swirl of dust
    and smoke.

And we—we followed in one long line, and it seemed like the
    end of things,
I know I'll never forget that charge, whatever the future
    brings!
I'm not much good at descriptive work. I haven't got much to
    tell;
But if ever you happen to get a whiff red-hot from the gates
    of Hell
You'll have a notion of what we struck, or the things we were
    stricken by:
Bullets and shrapnel and five-point-nines and bombs from the
    flaming sky.
Horses went over and men went down till it seemed there
    wasn't a hope
A single horseman would live to reach the foot of that shell-
    torn slope.

But it's hard for gunners to keep the range of cavalry moving fast,
And the fighting blood of the boys was up when we reached the redoubts at last.
Down we sprang with our bayonets fixed, and it wasn't left long in doubt;
I tell you those boys in the bush brigades could fight when you put them out.
We'd a score to settle long overdue; it was settled, you may depend.
Some Turks surrendered and others ran, but a few of them fought to the end.
A few of them fought to the bitter end, and whether we praise or blame,
Now that the whole thing's over and done; by God! there were some of them game!
Rightly or wrongly, they stuck to their guns when there wasn't a hope, they knew.
They fought like demons and died like men; and what more can a soldier do?

And Morgan? We found him at dawn of day—riddled with lead, of course—
Face up in front of the first redoubt and lying beside his horse.
His face had a sort of a peaceful smile it never had worn in life,
And we searched his tunic for letters and things to send them home to his wife.
And we found in a pocket just over his heart, a photo, torn in two—
And, somehow, or other, when I look back, I've a notion that Morgan knew!

By the Wady Imelaga

By the wady Imelaga, we were lying in reserve,
In a spot not far from Gaza, where the wady takes a curve.
We were planted in the hillocks snug and safe and out of sight,
While the Irish Tenth Division stormed the ridges on the right.

Underneath a hail of shrapnel we could see them marching past,
And they did not pause or falter, though their men were falling fast.
But the thing that gripped our fancy as we gazed upon the scene
Was the Irishman, who led them, holding high a flag of green.

Shells were bursting all around him and the shrapnel lashed the sand,
But he strode serenely onward with the banner in his hand,
While we held our breath and waited for a shot to lay him low
By the wady Imelaga on that evening long ago.

Young McDougall, who was resting with his elbows on the rise,
Started betting on the chances with the glasses to his eyes,
When a sniper somewhere handy sent a bullet through his brain
And his head dropped on the hillock, and he never moved again.

I was sorry for McDougall—he was such a cheerful soul.
Often I had ridden with him on the lonely night patrol.
And I started wondering, idly, who would be the next to go,
By the wady Imelaga when the sun was setting low.

How that picture haunts my mem'ry! I can see that barren hill
With the red blood trickling down it in a little, crimson rill,
And McDougall lying huddled with the glasses in his clutch.
Poor old Mac; you'd hardly credit that a man would bleed so much!

We had neither pick or shovel, but we had to do our best,
So we dug a grave with bayonets and we laid him down to rest,
And we heard the Irish shouting as they hurled upon the foe,
By the wady Imelaga on that evening long ago.

Twilight came, and darkness followed over mound and
    mosque and tomb,
As we rode away to northward in the silence and the gloom.
Far away the guns were calling, and the shrapnel stabbed
    the dark,
When we left McDougall lying, by the wady, cold and stark.

Oh, the war is now a mem'ry of the dim and distant past,
Old-time mates are half-forgotten, and old scenes are fading
    fast,
But that Irish standard-bearer, how he fared, I'd like to
    know,
By the wady Imelaga on that evening long ago.

The Brothers O'Brien

We were camped at Broadmeadows when war first began,
And with drilling and training fed-up to a man.
We were eager to sail and join in the fun
Of shooting the Turk and impaling the Hun,
Forgetting that much the same, laudable aim
Was inspiring the foe we were eager to tame;
When, early one day, with a yell and a whoop
The brothers O'Brien joined up with the troop.
Pat, Michael, and Dan, they were Irish indeed,
And pretty fair types of that turbulent breed;
Their figures were long and their tempers were short,
And there wasn't a thing from religion to sport
On which those three brothers could see eye to eye on,
It was war to the knife 'twixt the brothers O'Brien!
They soon became famous throughout the brigade,
For they argued on guard and they fought on parade,
They were always beginning or ending a fight—
Oh, the brothers O'Brien were Irish alright!

But if anyone else in the squadron should dare
To intrude, he would find 'twas a private affair.
Outsiders were barred, and if trouble began
They stood shoulder to shoulder, Pat, Michael, and Dan.
They were hefty and strong and as fierce as young lions,
And we learned to keep clear of the fighting O'Briens,

For many a trooper found out to his cost
That the brothers O'Brien refused to be bossed.

We sailed, and the vessel was hardly afloat
When an awful disturbance was heard on the boat.
We smiled, for we'd heard that commotion before,
It was just the O'Briens *discussing* the war.
But the language they used was both lurid and loose,
And it lasted right over with never a truce,
Till the regiment landed in Egypt, and then
The Pyramids started it over again!

They sent us to Anzac to settle the Turk,
And the brothers O'Brien got down to their work;
They were excellent shots, they were fired with zeal,
And many a Turk got a taste of their steel.
And it seemed the one subject on which they agreed
Was the Turk was a vile and a pestilent breed
That ought to be wiped off the face of the earth,
And they tried to achieve it for all they were worth!
But on frequent occasions in spite of it all
The brothers O'Brien found time for a brawl.

Alas for poor Dan! Life's a gamble at best;
He got a bit rash, and a Turk did the rest,
Reducing the brothers O'Brien to two...
They never said much, but they felt it, we knew.
O'er his grave they erected a little, rude cross,

And they set about grimly avenging his loss.
Then woe to the Moslem that Pat got his eye on,
Or who came in the road of his brother O'Brien!
Peace reigned in the troop for a fortnight at least,
And we thought the perpetual quarrel had ceased,
But 'twas only postponed as a tribute to Dan,
When the mourning was over, the fighting began!

Lone Pine finished Pat. In that fruitless attack
He was first o'er the top, and he never came back.
But he fought to the end as an Irishman should,
And his bayonet worked havoc as long as he stood,
And he slew enough Turks to escort him in pride
To the halls of Valhalla where heroes abide,
And I'm willing to bet when he landed across,
He found Dan was waiting—to argue the toss!

And Mick, poor old Mick, he was cut to the heart,
And he moped and he brooded alone and apart.
His brothers were gone, he had no more to lose,
He had no one to fight with, to punch or abuse.
Stagnation set in, and we mourned for the scion
Left lonely and sad of the house of O'Brien.
In the silence that followed, our souls seemed to droop,
And we longed for the sound of a row in the troop.
But, alas for poor Michael, the quarrel was o'er—
The brothers O'Brien would argue no more.

Mick fell at Romani, the last of them all,
And the last of the brothers to answer the call.
At the foot of a sandhill we laid him to rest,
And we felt in our hearts it was all for the best.
So ended the brothers, united in death,
As gallant a trio as ever drew breath,
And we knew that the squadron would mourn to a man
The fighting O'Briens, Pat, Michael, and Dan.

Now the war is long over—I hope it's the last—
But, at times, when I ponder and dream of the past,
My mem'ry goes back to that turbulent three:
The brothers O'Brien who could not agree.
And I think that St. Peter would not have the heart
To keep those three warrior brothers apart.
But if they're together, I'm willing to bet,
That the brothers O'Brien are arguing yet!

Song of the Sinai

Mates of the desert, the years have rolled and sundered the ties in twain
That bound us together in days of old, and only the dreams remain;
Only the dreams and a vague unrest, from the years that have fled so fast;
Like the sunset glory that gilds the west is the glory that gilds the past.
Fervent and strong was the faith we felt when our youthful hearts beat high,
And we rode to the jingle of spur and belt o'er the sands of the Sinai.

Do you remember that moonless hush on the white Romani sand,
When the Moslems came with a sudden rush and tackled us hand-to-hand?
Over the sandhills, wave on wave, they came ere the break of dawn;
Little quarter we got or gave as we met with our bayonets drawn.
"Allah, il Allah!" The echoes woke to the Moslem battle-cry,
And Mausers rattled and Maxims spoke on the sands of the Sinai.

On the hoof-stirred hillocks we came to grips, as the sun
   rose flaming red,
And some went West with a curse on their lips, and some
   with a prayer half-said.
But we smashed their centre and turned their flank, and
   drove them o'er ridge and *tel*,
And the day was won ere the red sun sank and the evening
   shadows fell.
By ridge and hillock the dead were strewn, and we left them
   there to lie,
And rode by the light of a crescent moon o'er the sands of
   the Sinai.

Branded and burned by the desert suns, drenched by the
   desert dew,
Ever we followed the sound of the guns o'er wastes where
   the wells were few.
Ever the mirage mocked our eyes on the pitiless path we
   trod,
And Death struck down from the brazen skies as swift as
   the wrath of God.
There were horses faltered and riders fell when the lead went
   whistling by,
And shrapnel blew like a breath from Hell o'er the sands of
   the Sinai.

Oh, there were nights when we cursed the foe, and bosom
    and brain grew numb,
When silence reigned and the moon sank low and we prayed
    for the day to come,
When our hopes grew faint and our goal seemed far, and
    our eyes grew misty and dim,
Till the dawn wind woke and the morning star rose over the
    skyline's rim.
But our faith revived and our fears took flight when the
    dawn suffused the sky,
And we rode away as the sun shone bright o'er the sands of
    the Sinai.

Mates of the desert, the tale is told, and the last crusade is
    o'er,
And the faith that gladdened our hearts of old is gone to
    return no more.
The seas are wide and the roads are long that sever us far
    apart,
But somewhere or other a random song may lighten a weary
    heart,
A lilting song of the days that were when our youthful
    hearts beat high,
And we rode to the jingle of belt and spur o'er the sands of
    the Sinai.

The Mother Speaks

I sat alone by the window seat
    On a morning long ago.
The winds were whispering cool and sweet
    And the swallows were skimming low.
And I saw you there, through the blinds half drawn,
    A picture of childish joy,
Standing at bay on the sunlit lawn,
    Waving a wooden toy.

You stood with your back to the garden-wall,
    And brandished your sword of wood,
And you rallied your men with a bugle-call
    As a brave commander should.
Ah, little we dreamed as we watched our sons,
    We mothers, that bright spring day,
How soon the music of distant guns
    Would be calling our boys away.

I watched you grow, as the years fled fast,
    To a stripling tall and strong,
Till the God of battles awoke at last
    From his slumber sound and long.
The drums were beating a wild tattoo,
    And the skies grew suddenly grey.
You were eager to answer the call, I knew—
    And how could I bid you stay?

The sky was dull, and the lawn was damp,
    And the world seemed all awry
On the last sad day of your leave from camp
    When we had to say good-bye.
But I smiled when the moment came to part,
    It was only to hide my pain,
For I knew deep down in my mother's heart
    That we would not meet again.

They brought me the message, alas, how brief!
    And I listened to them, dry-eyed.
Then crept to the attic to hide my grief
    Where your toys were laid aside.
They had felt the touch of your childish hand,
    They had shared in your childish glee,
And I felt, somehow, they would understand,
    Say nothing, and mourn with me.

I sit again by the window seat
    Where I sat long years ago.
The winds are whispering cool and sweet
    And the swallows are skimming low.
And I see again, through the blinds half drawn,
    A brave, little soldier boy,
Standing at bay on the sunlit lawn,
    Waving a wooden toy.

The Dead Come Home

Last night, when dozing in my room at midnight, dark and chill,
A sombre vision came to me that haunts my mem'ry still.
Within the silent city's heart I dreamed I stood alone
And heard the hour of midnight strike with mournful monotone,
And as the echoes died away I heard the tramp of feet
And saw the Army of the Dead come marching down the street.

They moved along with muffled tread, battalions and brigades,
Dead men who sang no battle songs, dead men who bore no blades.
Their uniforms were caked with mud and rent by shell and mine;
A crimson splash was on their brows, red laurels of the line.
Of ev'ry unit, ev'ry rank, of ev'ry creed and class,
United in the ranks of Death I saw the dead men pass.

I shuddered in my dream to see the dead come marching home
At midnight down the city street beneath the starry dome.
No banner waved above their heads; they passed in grim review,

And in those pallid ranks of death were many that I knew.
What brought them us at midnight hour; what came they
    here to seek?
And, lo! in answer to my prayer, I heard the dead men
    speak:—

"We are the mute, forgotten dead, the heroes of the line:
The men who fell on Anzac Beach, in France and Palestine;
From far Valhalla's lower halls where fallen fighters dwell
We come to see our native land and ask if all be well.
Our bones are scattered far and wide in many a lonely grave,
United now we come to see the land we died to save.

"For we have heard a murmur borne far muffled from below,
Across the barriers of death, the sounds of want and woe,
Of children crying out for bread while luxury and pride
Flaunt shamelessly on ev'ry hand. *Was it for this, we died?*
Is this the end for which we fought, the goal we died to
    gain?
Have all our sufferings gone for naught, and have we died in
    vain?

"We answered to the call to arms, unquestioning and blind,
We trusted to the promises of those we left behind.
We gave our lives ungrudgingly, we did not flinch nor quail,
Strong in the splendid faith we held that justice must prevail,
And as we drew our latest breath in sorrow and in pain,
This faith upheld us to the last: 'we do not die in vain.'

"We deemed that from our sacrifice a brighter world would rise,
Purged of the lust of greed and gain, a world more just and wise;
That peace would reign forever more between the warring Powers,
And happiness would smile again on this fair land of ours.
Till all your pledges to the dead are honoured and fulfilled
You're traitors to the faith we held whatever shrines you build!"

....

The ghostly regiments swept on, the murmur died away;
I woke to find the night was gone, the dawn was cold and grey.
A bitter rain was beating down upon my window-sill,
But in my brain I seemed to hear those ghostly voices still,
The voices of the noble dead repeating this refrain:
"Have all our sufferings gone for naught, and have we died in vain?"

Throwing Pebbles in the Sea

Brightly over bay and headland shines the early morning sun,
All the world is fresh and fragrant as if Time had just begun;
High o'er yonder rocky inlet where the morning mist still
    clings,
I can see the wild gulls wheeling with a flash of snow-white
    wings.
Far away on the horizon where the sky and ocean meet
Gleams on the spreading, trembling canvas of the home-
    bound fishing fleet.
Down below, the tide is rippling, and the waves are full of
    glee,
And all Nature seems to call me to a tryst beside the sea.

We are prone to be pretentious and to magnify our worth
As the monarchs of creation and the rulers of the earth,
But I seem to have a fancy as I watch those wheeling gulls
That it's just a fond delusion in our rather hollow skulls.
Not alone for us the sunshine, not alone for us the rain,
Not alone for us the glory of the mountain and the main.
We are only just some units in the great Creator's plan;
There are depths we cannot fathom, there are joys unknown
    to man.
Bounded by our dull horizon, slaves to precedent and form,
Can we feel the exultation of the gull that mounts the storm?

All the wisdom, all the learning we have garnered through
   the years
Have not stemmed the tide of sorrow or the flow of human
   tears.
Many hours I've spent in poring over dry philosophy,
But I might as well have spent them throwing pebbles in the
   sea.

It is but a foolish pastime fitted for an idle mind,
Still I'm rather prone to labours of an unproductive kind.
I remember as a youngster when I should have been at
   school
I would spend the summer morning throwing pebbles in the
   pool;
While the birds sang all around me and the wind sighed
   through the reeds,
I would watch the ripples spreading and I'd dream of
   mighty deeds.
All the world was then before me, fair and bright the future
   seemed;
Where are now the hopes I cherished; where are now the
   dreams I dreamed?

Gone! But in my heart I'll treasure mem'ries of those golden
   days
When that land of mine was bounded by a purple-tinted haze.
Oh! it helps me bear the burden of the evil days that be
Just to spend some idle moments throwing pebbles in the sea.

Comes a cool breeze from the ocean laden with the tang of
   brine,
And the gulls are wheeling seaward where they see the white
   wings shine.
At my feet, the waves are dancing, and they gurgle and they
   kiss;
Who would turn to musty volumes on a morning such as this?
There's more wisdom to be garnered from the earth and sea
   and sky
Than the sages ever dreamed of in the ages long gone by.
Nature is a kindly teacher, and she does not ask a fee
From a lonely, idle dreamer throwing pebbles in the sea.

Long ago on St. Helena lived an exile, sad and wan,
Brooding o'er the past, and mourning for his empire lost and
   gone.
Often, when the sun was setting, he would climb the rocky
   steep,
There to sit for hours and ponder, throwing pebbles in the deep.
He would muse and he would mutter as he watched the
   ripples spread,
Of the nations he had conquered, of the armies he had led.
But I like to think that, sometimes, when his thoughts began
   to roam
He would wander back in fancy to his happy childhood's home;
To the days ere glory called him from the island of his birth
To unleash the pent-up thunders and to shake the startled
   earth.

When his heart was gay and guileless, and he roamed, alone
    and free,
Round the rocky bays and inlets throwing pebbles in the sea.

Let the greedy strive for riches: it is but a selfish aim.
Let the soldier fight for glory, let the fool contend for fame.
Not within the gilded palace, not within the crowded mart
Can be found the balm and solace for an overburdened heart.
Vain are pomp and power and riches if the soul is not at peace;
Jason did not find contentment, though he found the golden
    fleece.
This is all I ask of heaven: let me dawdle on my way
Like a careless, happy pilgrim, living just from day to day,
And, at last, when all is over, this is my prayer, and this my
    plea:
Let me quietly sink to slumber like a pebble in the sea.

But the gulls are veering shoreward; I can see their white
    wings shine,
And a bank of cloud is rising on the far-off ocean line,
I have spent a pleasant hour moralising here alone,
And I know it's vain to worry over pleasures past and flown.
While the wind blows from the waters and the wild gulls
    wheel above,
I'll have something still to cherish, I'll have something still to
    love!
All the joys and all the sorrows that have been or are to be
Are as pebbles of the ocean, tiny ripples on the sea!

My Garden of Golden Dreams

I dwelt in a garden of golden dreams
    In the days when the world was new,
Midst verdant meadows and sparkling streams,
    And skies that were always blue.
Beautiful flowers and birds and bees
    Rejoiced in its sunny beams.
Oh, nothing was wanting to charm and please
    In my garden of golden dreams.

But I left my garden of dreams at length;
    I passed through the shining haze.
Forth I fared in my health and strength
    To wander by unknown ways.
The star of fortune above me shone—
    I followed its vagrant beams.
Like a will-o'-the-wisp, it lured me on
    From my garden of golden dreams.

I passed by many a mountain grand,
    Through forests sombre and lone.
I toiled and travelled by sea and land
    In many a clime and zone.
Till I wearied at length of the fruitless quest,
    Of the world and its sordid schemes,
And I longed for the flowers and perfect rest
    Of my garden of golden dreams.

Back I fared through the world again,
    Footsore, and faint and wan,
But I sought for my garden of dreams in vain—
    My garden of dreams was gone!
Gone forever the shining bowers,
    The meadows and sparkling streams.
For Time had withered the fragrant flowers
    In my garden of golden dreams.

Beautiful garden of golden dreams
    Set in a silver haze,
Happy were I could I dream the dreams
    I dreamt in those far-off days!
Beautiful flowers and birds and bees
    Rejoiced in its sunny beams.
Oh, nothing was wanting to charm or please
    In my garden of golden dreams.

A Random Shaft

I only spoke the words in jest;
    I could have bitten off my tongue,
To see the arrow pierce your breast,
    To mark how bitterly it stung.

The blood drained slowly from your cheek
    As tides ebb backward from the shore.
I saw, and yet I dare not speak,
    Lest speaking, I offend the more.

You fought, you faltered, gained control,
    The blood came back to cheek and brow,
But ah; the secret of your soul
    To me was not a secret now!

And yet, it fills me with surprise
    To think a shallow doll like her,
With powdered cheeks and pencilled eyes,
    A soul so deep as yours could stir!

But who am I to judge her so?
    Perhaps your clearer eyes may see
Beneath the powder and the show
    A beauty that is veiled to me.

Unconscious bias warps the mind.
    We'd rather censure than condone
The faults and frailties that we find
    In other natures than our own.

Howe'er it be, with all my heart,
    When I recall your look of pain,
I wish I had not winged the dart
    That made an old wound bleed again.

The Girl in the Street

The form of a goddess, the face of a saint,
With a tint in her hair that no artist could paint.
She trips down the sidewalk alluring and sweet;
The pavement Madonna: the girl in the street.

So queenly her carriage, so perfect her poise,
She vexes the matrons and gladdens the boys.
And even the constable pacing his beat,
Has a nod and a smile for the girl in the street.

Bewitchingly bold, yet alluringly coy,
Not Mary of Scotland, nor Helen of Troy
For the favour of princes would dare to compete
With this blue-eyed Madonna, this girl in the street.

Oh, the foolish may sneer, and the godly may frown,
But I swear she's a queen, though she hasn't a crown.
From the top of her head to her dear little feet,
She is Empress of Beauty, the girl in the street.

Though she may not behave just as well as she should,
Her eyes are so deep that I know she is good,
And there's many a lady among the élite,
May envy the lot of the girl in the street.

Yet I own I am worried and troubled at times,
For how can a penniless peddler of rhymes,
Who has nothing to spend and but little to eat,
Watch over this exquisite queen of the street.

It's a callous old world, and I'm rather afraid
That some shadow may fall on this bright little maid.
So I murmur a prayer ev'ry time that we meet
That the fates will be kind to the girl in the street.

But a voice in my ear like the voice of an elf
Seems to whisper: "that girl can look after herself."
And the devil himself would be glad to retreat
If he tried any tricks on this girl in the street.

Pedigree

Some people boast an awful lot about their pedigree,
But I am not at all concerned about my family tree.
They must have been a varied lot, the sires from whom I
    sprung;
I shouldn't be at all surprised if some of them were hung!
No doubt they stretch a long way back, as families mostly
    do,
But how they lived, or what they did, I've not the slightest
    clue.
And even if I knew them all right back to Noah's Ark,
I'm game to lay a shade of odds I'd keep the matter dark.

There might have been a king or two upon my father's side,
A Cœur de Lion or Robert Bruce to raise the family pride,
A man of courage and resource who pressed towards his goal,
Nor ever worried overmuch for his immortal soul;
Who grabbed whatever he could grab, and ate and drank his
    fill,
And brushed his enemies aside or bent them to his will.
If such a one to me were kin—a Tudor or a Guelph,
His blood is running very thin in my degenerate self.

There might have been a pirate too, a Morgan or a Kidd,
Who made his victims walk the plank, as pirates mostly did;
A fierce, freebooting, reckless knave, who made his presence felt,
A crimson cutlass in his hand, a pistol in his belt;
Who lorded it in tavern bars and quaffed the blazing rum,
And sent all foes who crossed his path non-stop to Kingdom Come.
I hope that there was such a one, for, though I hate the sea,
I'd like to think I had a drop of pirate blood in me!

There might have been—but what's the use?—for when you come to think,
It's plain enough we all evolved from Darwin's missing link.
And, though we've long since lost our tails and changed a bit in shape,
We're only monkeys more or less—a sort of super-ape.
So if you have a friend who boasts, just use a bit of tact,
And when he speaks of high descent, remind him of the fact.
For, after all is said and done, it's plain as plain can be,
We can't afford to brag too much about our pedigree.

Socrates

I sometimes wish that I had lived
    In Athens, long ago,
When Socrates, that grand old sage,
    Went gadding to and fro,
Interrogating all he met,
    Especially the youths,
In zealous search of moral laws,
    And universal truths.

Though pestered by a nagging wife
    And debts and other woes,
He never faltered in his search
    Or quailed before his foes.
He was too wise and good a man
    To quarrel with his spouse,
So when an argument occurred,
    He simply left the house.

Though not at all of god-like mien,
    Round-bellied, like a cask,
A mighty spirit lurked beneath
    That queer Silenus mask.
All Athens knew the grand, old sage
    With bare, unsandalled feet,
Who quizzed and questioned all he met
    In market-place and street.

He treated friends and foes alike,
    He took them all to task,
Prepared at all times to propound,
    To answer or to ask.
He tore their arguments to shreds
    And left them all at sea.
He turned the sophists inside out
    With gentle irony.

And when before the festal board
    He sat and drank his fill,
No man in Athens could withstand
    His dialectic skill.
Though others grew bemused with drink
    And rolled beneath the board,
Stout Socrates drank calmly on
    And talked while others snored.

He was a gallant soldier too,
    As manfully he proved;
When others fled, he stood his ground,
    Unruffled and unmoved.
He saved young Alcibiades,
    His wild Athenian friend,
For whom remorseless fate reserved
    A more ignoble end.

So Socrates went calmly on,
    Serene and unafraid,
And when he heard the inner voice
    He hearkened and obeyed.
Unstirred alike by praise or blame,
    By censure or applause,
He probed deep to the heart of things
    In quest of moral laws.

And when at last before the court
    He stood erect and proud,
He scorned to truckle to his foes
    Or pander to the crowd.
He spoke with matchless eloquence,
    And put them all to shame.
He proved that virtue was his goal
    And truth his only aim.

But hate and ignorance prevailed,
    The fatal vote was cast,
Though many of his noble friends
    Were faithful to the last.
He calmly bade them all farewell,
    Then drained the hemlock bowl,
And passed into the Great Unknown
    Serene and calm of soul.

Now, sometimes, when I lie awake,
    Depressed and ill at ease,
It cheers my drooping soul to think
    Of grand, old Socrates.
Who lived to teach the larger truths
    That meaner souls deny,
And show how well a man may live,
    How nobly he may die.

Slander

We all fear the serpent that lurks in the grass
And strikes with his poisonous fangs as we pass.
But a deadlier menace to old and to young
Is the venom that drips from a slanderous tongue!

Cradle Song

I heard a mother singing, singing very soft and low
To her baby in the cradle as she rocked it to and fro.
Twilight shades were falling round me but I stayed my steps to hear,
And I bowed my head in silence for I knew that God was near.

I was weary and dejected, one I loved had done me wrong,
But my heart was touched and softened by the mother's cradle song.
And the bitter thoughts I harboured fled like magic from my soul
As the accents of the mother to my inmost being stole.

And I stood there list'ning, list'ning till the song to silence fell,
And the child was hushed to slumber and I knew that all was well;
Then I went my way rejoicing. Love is tender, love is strong;
Heav'n will hold no sweeter music than a mother's cradle song.

The Quiet Folk

I spent to-day with the quiet folk
    Who dwell in a place apart,
Far from the beat of hurrying feet
    And the hum of the crowded mart.
Their homes are set on the silent hill
    Where the tall pines nod and sway,
Where sparrows twitter and pigeons coo
    Through the livelong, summer day.

You may speak if you will to the quiet folk
    But will only waste your breath,
For they lie fast bound in a trance profound,
    A slumber known as death.
It's little they care for the sigh or prayer,
    The cross or the mouldering wreath,
For nothing troubles the quiet folk
    In their cosy beds beneath.

I sometimes think of the quiet folk
    In the midnight dark and chill,
When I lie awake, and the windows shake,
    And the rain beats on the sill.
Where they lie asleep in their chambers deep,
    From care and sorrow freed,
In the calm democracy of death
    That knows no class nor creed.

Some day I will dwell with the quiet folk,
    And I will be silent too,
When I lie in the shade of the pine-tree glade
    Where the pigeons bill and coo.
Sorrow or care will not reach me there.
    I will sleep and dream my fill
When I lie at last with the quiet folk
    On the slope of the pine-clad hill.

The Kerrigan Boys

By Jove! it's hot on the track to-day; my flannel is soaked
  with sweat.
I think I'll sit in the shade a bit and wait for the sun to set.
I know of a decent camping place by the river beyond the
  town,
And I'd rather carry my swag through there after the sun
  goes down.

A touch of pride? Well, perhaps it is, though I haven't much
  cause for pride.
It's sixteen years to a day almost since old man Kerrigan
  died;
Sixteen years, and his place is sold, and the fortune he left us
  spent!
Well, the road downhill is an easy road, and that was the
  way we went.

Kerrigan, that was our father's name, was one of the tough,
  old sort;
He held by graft as he held by God, and he hated drink and
  sport.
We lads were fond of a bit of fun, but he kept us under the
  rein,
And we had to bow to the old man's will though it went
  against our grain.

He was kind enough in his grim, old way, but we had to
    earn our keep,
Driving horses and milking cows, branding and shearing
    sheep.
No wonder we bucked a bit at times, for you know what
    youngsters are.
We mustn't dance at the local hall or drink in Mulligan's bar.

Well, those were the orders the old man gave, but we did it
    just the same.
Jack was two years younger than I, so I was the more to
    blame.
But I've often thought had he been less hard and left us a bit
    more free
It might have been better for him, perhaps, and better for
    Jack and me.

The old man dropped in the yard one day where we had the
    weaners penned,
We picked him up and we carried him home, but we knew
    that it was the end.
The neighbours gathered for miles around; he hadn't a single
    foe,
And the crowd that stood by the open grave spoke well for
    the man below.

We grieved a lot for the old man's death, though he left us
    wealthy men,
If we had not known what he meant to us, we realised it
    then.
Our only sister had died at birth, and our mother was long
    since dead,
And we found that we were the only heirs when the old
    man's will was read.

We were just a couple of country lads, we had never been off
    the farm,
We'd been held in check from our boyhood up by the weight
    of the old man's arm;
Good in saddle, and fair with our fists, with a touch of the
    old man's pride,
But the neighbours muttered and shook their heads when
    old man Kerrigan died.

Hard and all as the old man was, for years he had kept a
    stud,
For the love of a horse for the horse's sake is strong in the
    Irish blood.
But breeding was only a hobby with him, a sort of harmless
    craze,
Though I sometimes fancied he'd had his fling 'way back in
    his younger days!

We got mixed up with a racing crowd, and started to go the pace;
We forgot the sound of the old man's voice and the frown on his rugged face.
For the road downhill is an easy road, though it ends in a swift descent;
We were only youngsters, a reckless pair—and that was the way we went.

We staked for a win on the Chester colt on the strength of a trial he showed,
But someone got to the boy on top—we knew by the race he rode.
He lost ten lengths and he finished last. It was useless to make a fuss;
For the men we met in the racing game were *far* too cunning for us!

We backed him again in the Greytown Cup and he won by half the straight,
But we left our cash in the bookies' bags, for he failed to draw the weight.
We cursed the jockey, we cursed the horse, and we sold him there and then,
We'd had enough of the racing game and the ways of racing men!

We could have got out of our troubles still if we'd put our
    hands to the plough,
But the life of leisure, and cards and drink, had got the grip
    on us now.
You may call it flashness, or call it pride, or simply a want of
    sense,
But the publicans, and the auctioneers, grew wealthy at our
    expense.

We sat and drank in Mulligan's pub, and gambled the whole
    night long.
We dealt in cattle, we dealt in sheep, and most of our deals
    went wrong.
As long as the bank would cash our cheques we didn't care
    what we spent,
For the road downhill is an easy road, and that was the way
    we went.

Then things got bad, and a drought came on, and it lasted
    over a year.
Our dams gave out and our stock died off, and we knew
    that the end was near.
Our credit stopped and the bank foreclosed, and our father's
    place was sold.
For the road downhill is an easy road as the Prodigal found
    of old.

Five years after the old man's death together we took the track;
We swagged it into the nearest town, and I had a drink with Jack.
Then he shook my hand and he wished me luck; I knew he was close to tears,
And I've never set eyes on Jack since then, or heard of him now for years.

Somewhere out to the west of Bourke he's humping his swag maybe,
Tramping along in the broiling sun and cursing himself and me.
I'd give two years of my worthless life, though it may not last that long,
For one more look in his honest face, one grip of his fingers strong.

Well, that's the tale of the Kerrigan boys, and the moral is near the end:
You'll always have plenty of friends at hand *as long as you've cash to spend!*
We had our chance and we played the fool, and it's too late now to repent,
For the road downhill is an easy road, and that was the way we went.

The Bushrangers

"The historic Faithful Creek homestead, where the Kelly gang held their prisoners while they robbed the bank at Euroa, has been destroyed by fire."

—News Item.

Four horsemen rode out from the heart of the range,
Four horsemen with aspects forbidding and strange.
They were booted and spurred, they were armed to the teeth,
And they frowned as they looked on the valley beneath,
As forward they rode through the rocks and the fern—
Ned Kelly, Dan Kelly, Steve Hart and Joe Byrne.

Ned Kelly drew rein and he shaded his eyes—
"The town's at our mercy! See yonder it lies!
To hell with the troopers!"—he shook his clenched fist—
"We will shoot them like dogs if they dare to resist!"
And all of them nodded, grim-visaged and stern—
Ned Kelly, Dan Kelly, Steve Hart and Joe Byrne.

Through the gullies and creeks they rode silently down.
They stuck up the station and raided the town;
They opened the safe and they looted the bank.
They laughed and were merry, they ate and they drank.
Then off to the ranges they went with their gold—
Oh! never were bandits more reckless and bold.

But time brings its punishment, time travels fast,
And the outlaws were trapped in Glenrowan at last,
Where three of them died in the smoke and the flame,
And Ned Kelly came back—to the last he was game.
But the Law shot him down (he was fated to hang),
And that was the end of the bushranging gang.

Whatever their faults and whatever their crimes,
Their deeds lend romance to those faraway times.
They have gone from the gullies they haunted of old,
And nobody knows where they buried their gold.
To the ranges they loved they will never return—
Ned Kelly, Dan Kelly, Steve Hart and Joe Byrne.

But at times when I pass through that sleepy old town
Where the far-distant peaks of Strathbogie look down,
I think of the days when those grim ranges rang
To the galloping hoofs of the bushranging gang.
Though the years bring oblivion, time brings a change—
The ghosts of the Kellys still ride from the range.

My Old Black Billy

I have humped my bluey in all the States
With my old black billy, the best of mates.
For years I have camped, and toiled, and tramped
On roads that are rough and hilly,
With my plain and sensible,
Indispensable,
Old black billy.

My old black billy, my old black billy,
Whether the wind is warm or chilly
I always find when the shadows fall
My old black billy, the best mate of all.

I have carried my swag on the parched Paroo
Where water is scarce and the houses few,
On many a track, in the great Out Back
Where the heat would drive you silly
I've carried my sensible,
Indispensable,
Old black billy.

When the days of tramping at last are o'er
And I drop my swag at the Golden Door,
Saint Peter will stare when he sees me there.
Then he'll say "Poor wandering Willie,
Come in with your sensible,
Indispensable,
Old black billy."

The Tarra Valley

In the heart of the hills there's a valley I know,
And its memory haunts me wherever I go;
Though far have I wandered by land or by sea,
That little green valley is Eden to me.
There's a road winding down, and it twists and it turns
To sweet Tarra Valley, the valley of ferns.

There at morning the magpie sings clear as a flute,
And seldom the chime of the bellbird is mute.
And at night when the valley is lit by the moon
The swans flying westward go by with a croon,
And the light like a star in the small window burns
Of a little red house in the valley of ferns.

There's balm for all sorrows, a cure for all ills
In that little green valley away in the hills;
For my sweetheart lives there, and, when daylight is o'er,
She watches and waits by the vine-covered door.
So I'm going back home when the springtime returns
To dear Tarra Valley, the valley of ferns.

The Red Steer

When the wind has blown from the North for days
And the smoke clouds denser grow,
When the sun is veiled by a blood-red haze
And the rivers and creeks are low,
Oh, that is the time of the fierce, red steer,
The season of drought and dread,
And the bushmen gather from far and near
When the distant sky grows red.
For there's death before and there's death behind
When the red steer gallops before the wind.

In the hot midday or the dead of night
With a bellowing sound he comes,
And the skies are filled with a ghastly light
As he roars through the ferns and gums.
Over river and ridge and creek
He flies in his fierce career,
And it's woe alike to the strong and weak
Who meet with the fierce, red steer.
He has no mercy on old or young
With his flaming breath and his lolling tongue.

A hush of terror, a sense of doom
Broods over the lofty range.
The settler peers through the gathering gloom
And prays for the wind to change.
In lonely huts where the children sleep,
And on many an Out Back farm
The brave bush mothers their vigils keep
Filled with a vague alarm
When the midnight heavens grow weird and strange,
And the red steer gallops across the range.

He gives no quarter, he makes no truce
As the settler knows too well,
And he who would set the red steer loose
Is a fiend direct from hell!
So guard your forests; they're yours to guard.
Post sentinels far and near,
Lest the hills and valleys again be scarred
By the hoofs of the fierce, red steer.
You must watch by night, you must watch by day
To keep the fierce, red steer at bay!

Drover's Song

We are droving down the Lachlan with a mob of starving sheep,
And we're sometimes short of tucker, and we lose a lot of sleep,
For there's fifteen thousand wethers and as many ewes and lambs,
And the drought has burned the stock-routes and dried up the creeks and dams,
But a drover can't be worried over little things like that,
We must keep the mob a-moving whether they are lean or fat.

The squatters see us coming, and they grumble as we pass,
For they swear we break their fences and eat up the station grass,
But our boss, an old-time drover, has been at the game for years;
He can talk to angry squatters and stand up to overseers,
For there's always something doing with a straggling, starving mob.
You must get them feed and water, and you've got to do your job!

Oh, the farmer to the plough, and the sailor to the sea,
But the droving life, the roving life, is the only life for me,
For you see a lot of country and you have a lot of fun,
And the girls are always waiting when our droving trip is done.

Yes, it's pleasant when you're camping underneath the
   western stars,
And the evening winds are sighing through the gums and
   green belars,
Just to sit and yarn together round the brightly blazing logs
While the weary mob is resting guarded by the watchful
   dogs.
Ah, it's grand to wake at morning to the magpie's merry call;
Oh, the careless, droving, roving life is the finest life of all!

The Fossicker

"There's gold in the ranges," the fossicker said,
  Wistfully shaking his old, grey head
  As he gazed away at the distant peaks.
"There's gold in the gullies and dried-up creeks,
  But I'm much too weak and I'm far too old
  To climb the ranges in search of gold.

"But if I were younger," he stroked his brow,
"The sort of youngster that you are now,
  I'd be off tomorrow with spade and dish;
  What grander life could a young man wish?
  When the blood is warm and the heart is bold,
  Oh, *that* is the season to search for gold!

"I fossick a bit in the creeks around,
  But the gold is lying in higher ground.
  There are hills to climb, there are creeks to ford
  Before you come to the golden hoard.
  You must face the hunger, and heat, and cold,
  But I know that the ranges are full of gold.

"But I'm not as young as I used to be,
  And whoever finds it, it won't be me!
  For I'm too old now, but I know it's there;
  One stroke of the shovel will lay it bare."
  Then his voice grew shrill, and he cried:
"Behold!"—
  Lo; the peaks were flushed with the sunset gold.

Old Timer

Sitting alone by the blazing fire,
Thoughtfully puffing your old, black briar,
Dreaming away to your heart's content
Of the sheds you rung and the cheques you spent
In the far-off days when your eye was bright,
Your pocket was full and your heart was light,
When you worked all day and you danced all night,
Old Timer!

Little you cared for the rain or mud,
A pitch-black night or a creek in flood,
With a horse to ride and a cheque to spend,
And a drink and a dance at the journey's end,
Where red lips pouted and soft hands clung
And the fiddles squeaked and the dancers swung.
Ah! those were the days when your heart was young,
Old Timer!

When a colt unbroken or maid unkissed
Was a challenge your heart could not resist,
And your shapely nose was a trifle marred
When, stripped to the pelt in the shanty yard,
You fought it out to the bitter end
With the six-foot bully of Boundary Bend
Who cast a slur on your absent friend,
Old Timer!

So busy with stockwhip and axe and shears,
You hardly noticed the passing years
Till your beard was grey and you woke to find
That somehow or other you'd dropped behind;
And the girls you had flirted and danced with then
Got married or drifted beyond your ken,
And you couldn't keep pace with the younger men,
Old Timer!

But what does it matter? You did your best,
And if life lacks most of its old-time zest,
There'll be Someone waiting to ease your load
When you reach the end of the Sunset Road.
Now all you need is a well-filled briar,
A cosy chair and a blazing fire,
To doze and dream to your heart's desire,
Old Timer!

The Girl of the Range

The girl of the ranges, you know her, of course,
With her long golden hair, and her bonny black horse.
She gallops at morning and gallops at night.
Oh, the girl of the ranges is swift in her flight.

Refrain:
Girl of the range, girl of the range,
Wild as a plover, untutored and strange,
She will bid you goodbye with a toss of her head,
For the girl of the range is unwooed and unwed.

Oh, the bushmen may laugh, or the bushmen may sigh,
When they see the wild girl of the ranges go by,
But a wave of her hand, and a click of the spurs,
And all the wide range of the mountains is hers.

I have followed her fast, through the bracken and fern,
O'er creeks and o'er gullies; but only to learn
That wild as the wind is, and swifter than thought,
The girl of the ranges can never be caught.

"There's Only Two of Us Here"

I camped one night in an empty hut on the side of a lonely hill;
I didn't go much on empty huts, but the night was awful chill.
So I boiled me billy and had me tea, and seen that the door was shut,
Then I went to bed in an empty bunk by the side of the old slab hut.

It must have been about twelve o'clock—I was feeling cosy and warm—
When at the foot of me bunk I sees a horrible ghostly form.
It seemed in shape to be half an ape with a head like a chimpanzee,
But wot the 'ell was it doin' there, and wot did it want with me?

You may say if you please that I had d.ts. or call me a crimson liar,
But I wish you had seen it as plain as me with its eyes like coals of fire!
Then it gave a moan and a horrible groan that curdled me blood with fear,
And, "There's only two of us here," it ses; "there's only two of us here!"

I kept one eye on the old hut door and one on the awful brute;
I only wanted to dress meself and get to the door and scoot.
But I couldn't find where I'd left me boots so I hadn't a chance to clear;
And, "There's only two of us here," it moans, "there's only two of us here!"

I hadn't a thing to defend meself, not even a stick or stone;
And, "There's only two of us here!" it ses again with a horrible groan.
I thought I'd better make some reply, though I reckoned me end was near:
"By the holy smoke, when I finds me boots there'll be only one of us here!"

I gets me hands on me number tens and out through the door I scoots,
And I lit the whole of the hillside up with the sparks from me blucher boots.
So I've never slept in a hut since then, and I tremble and shake with fear
When I think of that horrible form wot moaned, "There's only two of us here!"

The Swagman's Song

I'm just an old swaggie, I have no home,
But I carry my swag wherever I roam.
The squatters may frown and the cooks may abuse
But I pitch my camp wherever I choose.
For I must have grub, and baccy, and beer,
And I'm always handy when night is near.

I am lulled to sleep by the night wind's sigh,
The mopoke's call and the curlew's cry.
I wake at morn to the magpie's song,
And I boil my billy by the billabong.

I'm just an old swaggie, I have no friend,
And it's just an old swaggie I'll be to the end.
I know all the squatters, I know all the cooks,
And it's little I care for their surly looks.
So I have no trouble and I have no fear,
But I'm always handy when night is near.

When I come at last to my journey's end
You can lay me to rest in some quiet bend
And carve these verses above my grave:
"He was no man's master, and no man's slave,
But he liked good baccy, he liked his beer,
And now he is taking his last rest here."

Lasseter's Last Long Ride

Lasseter rode from his camping-ground
    As the sun sank low in the west,
But who can say what Lasseter found,
    Or what was Lasseter's quest?
Others will go where the fierce winds blow
    And try as Lasseter tried,
But only God and the white stars know
    The end of Lasseter's ride.

The desert waste is a burning waste
    And thirst is a bitter goad.
He must ride in darkness and ride in haste
    On the track that Lasseter rode;
With never a mate to share his fate
    And never a peak to guide,
For only God and the stars looked down
    On Lasseter's last long ride.

Now Lasseter lies in the great north-west
    Where they say that the dead sleep sound,
But what was the end of Lasseter's quest,
    And where is the gold he found?
He rode alone to the great unknown
    And followed a phantom guide,
For only God and the stars looked down
    On Lasseter's last long ride.

Oh, some may jest at his fruitless quest,
    Or murmur his name in grief,
But, somewhere, out in the great north-west
    Lies Lasseter's golden reef.
And men will track to the great Out Back
    And die, as Lasseter died,
For only God and the stars looked down
    On Lasseter's last long ride.

Banjo

Andrew Barton Paterson, Australian poet, known far and wide by his pen-name of "The Banjo," died on February 5th, 1941, at 77 years of age.

—News Item.

Don't tell me that "The Banjo's" dead—oh, yes, I've heard the tale—
But "Banjo" isn't dead at all, he's caught the western mail.
He has a lot of friends, you know, among the western men,
He wants to look into their eyes and grip their hands again;
He longs to spend some quiet nights beneath the western stars
And hear the evening wind again among the green belars.
So if they tell you "Banjo's" dead just say that it's a lie:
He comes from where they breed 'em tough and "Banjo" will not die.

They say that Clancy sent him word, he's at the Overflow
With many more old mates of his who knew him long ago.
The man from Snowy River's there from Kosciusko's side
Who brought the wild mob in alone and showed them how to ride.
He's got his mountain pony, too, as tough and wiry yet
As when he chased the brumby mob and colt from old Regret.
Another chap—now, what's his name? He comes from Ironbark—
He thought the barber cut his throat and didn't like the lark.

All these old mates of his are there, with others on the way,
And when he got a call from them, well—how could "Banjo" stay?
There's Gundagai and Saltbush Bill, a rough and rugged pair—
I bet that there will be some fun when "Banjo" meets them there.
Old Trooper Scott is coming, too, to represent the force,
And Andy Regan (or his ghost) on Father Riley's horse.
They're making for the Overflow, and when they all arrive
You'll see that "Banjo" isn't dead, he's very much alive.

They'll hold a racing match of course—you bet your life they will!
And there'll be fun with Gundagai and tough old Saltbush Bill.
Old Pardon will be hard to beat—they say he knows the track—
But Swagman p'raps may run him close with Ryan on his back.
And, near at hand, old Rio Grande is sure to make a claim,
With bold Macpherson riding hard, a horseman grim and game.
I see them racing neck and neck, and as they near the post
Old Faugh-a-Ballagh hits the front with Regan (or his ghost).

Old Faugh-a-Ballagh hits the front, but as they pass the judge
A yell goes up for Mongrel Grey, the poor old station drudge
(Who, with the boy strapped on his back, through swirling flood and foam,
Swam bravely through the pitch-black night to bring the youngster home).
Old Mongrel Grey has beat 'em all, an honest horse and true,
And Clancy's glad to see him win, and so is "Banjo," too.

Then glasses clink, and healths are drunk, and many a tale is told
Of roving days and droving days that never will grow old.
The seasons come, the seasons go, and little here abides,
But good old "Banjo" will not die as long as Clancy rides.
As long as bushmen love a horse or wild, black swans go by,
As long as there's a Southern Cross "The Banjo" will not die.
So send the joyous news abroad, through hut and shearing shed,
And tell the bushmen not to grieve, *for "Banjo" is not dead!*

Port Noarlunga

On the beach at Port Noarlunga
    When the skies were dull and grey,
Long ago we met together,
    You, to go, and I, to stay.
Overhead, the gulls were wheeling,
    And the tide was flowing free
On the beach at Port Noarlunga,
    Port Noarlunga by the sea.

London called, and you made answer,
    There your voice would bring you fame,
But my heart grew cold within me
    When the hour of parting came.
It would not be long, you murmured,
    You would come again to me,
I must wait at Port Noarlunga,
    Port Noarlunga by the sea.

On the beach at Port Noarlunga
    Year by year I watched and yearned,
But no more to Port Noarlunga
    Have your wandering footsteps turned.
I am weary, I am lonely,
    This my prayer, and this my plea:
Come you back to Port Noarlunga,
    Port Noarlunga by the sea.

The Derelicts

There's a winter's night in the years long flown
That is stamped indelibly on my mind,
When I wandered forth in the dark alone
Burning with hatred for all mankind,
And I longed for talons that I might rend
The heart of a foe I had deemed a friend.

Down a desolate street I went
With an aching heart and an empty purse,
An outcast Adam with shoulders bent
Under the weight of the primal curse,
When out of the shadows, uncouth and lame,
A homeless dog from the darkness came.

He stopped beside me and wagged his tail
And looked at me in a wistful way
With a look so human I could not fail
To understand what he meant to say:
"There's a bond of mateship between us two.
I am a derelict, so are you."

He must have come from a secret lair,
It was plain enough that he had no home,
For his big lop ears and his long, brown hair
Had never been touched by a brush or comb.
But he looked at me with his big moist eyes
And I knew he wanted to sympathise.

A woman or man may be false or true,
But this we know since the world began,
Though friends turn traitors and foes pursue,
A dog will stick to a hunted man,
And few will shelter or few forgive
The homeless dog or the fugitive.

He was a derelict, so was I,
Down-and-outs who had met by chance.
Policemen paused as we passed them by
And eyed us both with a searching glance,
For the law is ever alert to scan
A homeless dog or a homeless man.

We came to a restaurant crammed with food,
Eggs, and poultry, and pork, and fish,
Fried, or roasted, or boiled, or stewed,
All that a dog or a man might wish.
The tables were set and the doors flung wide,
But no one asked us to go inside.

Jewelled ladies, superbly dressed,
Pampered pets of the social clan,
Passed us by with a laugh or jest,
A homeless dog and a homeless man.
But we did not ask them for sympathy;
I was hungry and so was he.

The door of the chapel before us shone,
A priest was preaching of vice and sin,
But we seemed to feel that our chance had gone,
And no one asked us to enter in.
What hope had we at the Pearly Gate—
A homeless dog and his homeless mate?

The night was bitter, and so were we.
On we passed through the night and fog,
And we mused how callous the world can be
To a homeless man and a homeless dog.
The lethal chamber, the prison van
For the homeless dog and the homeless man.

We climbed 'way up to the lonely park
In search of shelter—a dismal pair.
We camped in a corner, obscure and dark,
With only our sorrows and woes to share.
Ishmaels under a social ban—
A homeless dog and a homeless man.

We lost each other next day again
In the self-same street we had met before.
I looked for hours but looked in vain.
The city had swallowed you up once more.
But I met a friend as I searched for you,
Who helped me, cheered me, and pulled me through.

Brave, old mate with the eyes of brown,
You have long since gone from the earth I know
To a warm, bright kennel with beds of down
Where the souls of all lonely and lost dogs go,
Where none may enter to stone or flog,
Or scold or harass a hungry dog.

And there reposing in blissful state
With friends in plenty and food to spare,
You have long forgotten the old time mate
Who tramped with you through the cold night air,
Forlorn and friendless and chilled to the bone,
To camp the night in the park alone.

But I'll remember till life shall end,
The night, the silence, the drifting fog,
That bitter night when I found a friend,
And I learned this much from a homeless dog:
To tend and shelter whene'er I can
A homeless dog or a homeless man.

O'Brien's Leap

'Twas Friday night in Murphy's pub, and seated round the fire
Was Joe Magee, and Bourke, and me, and Mick O'Brien the liar.
When someone asked the greatest height a man had ever cleared
O'Brien looked into the flames and stroked his long, grey beard.

"Just listen for awhile," he said, "I'll settle all disputes.
The greatest jump this world has known was done in blucher boots!
It happened many years ago when I was on the spree
That night I jumped the graveyard fence." He looked at Joe Magee.

"I'd blued me cheque at Guinan's pub, a cheque of fifty quid—
You youngsters cannot sink the beer like us old timers did!
The graveyard stood across the road, a stone-throw from the bar;
I wandered in and fell asleep. You know what graveyards are.

"It ain't a pleasant place to wake at midnight all alone,
And I was lyin' on a grave, me head against a stone.
A thunderstorm had just gone by and soaked me to the pelt.
You'll have to knock down fifty quid to feel the way I felt!

"I rose meself and looked around; I tried to pierce the gloom—
A big, stone cross was on me left, and on me right, a tomb.
A great, black pine-tree spread above, and, as its branches swayed,
A bough stretched down, and, like a hand, it touched me shoulder-blade.

"Jehosephat! I gave a yell; the graveyard fence was near
With big, spiked railings eight foot high a greyhound couldn't clear.
I bounded up into the air—you never seen the likes!
But—curse me luck!—me blucher boots got jammed between the spikes!

"Instead of landing on me feet, I landed on me phiz—
You'll have to get a scare like me to know what jumpin' is!
The ground outside was rather soft (you jokers needn't laugh!)
And there beside that graveyard fence I left me photograph!

"No matter how a fellow talks, there's blokes you *can't* convince.
But them there bluchers weighed me down—I've never worn 'em since.
I took a set on graveyards too." He looked into the blaze,
"And cheques of fifty quid," he sighed, "are hard to get these days.

"But if you talk of jumping feats with ignorant galoots,
Just say O'Brien's mighty leap was done in *blucher boots!*
That night he jumped the graveyard fence—a leap of eight foot clear—
Weighed down by flamin' blucher boots and full of Guinan's beer!"

The Girl with the Pram

Victoria Markets are crowded tonight,
And I'm rather confused by the glare and the light
As I'm jostled and pushed between barrow and stall,
And I rather regret that I came here at all
As I wander around like a motherless lamb,
Till I get in the wake of the girl with the pram.

Onward she sails like a boat through the blue.
She opens a path and I follow her through,
Cleaving the crowd as the ocean is cleft,
She flings them aside to the right and the left.
Little she cares for the crush and the jam,
They've *got* to make way for the girl with the pram!

A moment she halts for a dialogue brief
In front of the stall of an almond-eyed thief
Who tries to dispose of some lettuce and thyme,
And carrots and cabbages well past their prime.
Then she tosses her head and she mutters a "Damn!"
And onward she charges, the girl with the pram.

Nothing can hinder her headlong career.
I follow behind her a bit in the rear,
Like a rowing boat towed by a liner at sea;
(I'm mixing my metaphors somewhat maybe!)
But the crowd is so dense that it's lucky I am
To be safe in the wake of the girl with the pram.

She stops by a swarthy-cheeked son of the South,
And I catch just a glimpse of her humorous mouth
As she looks at the fruits and the products displayed.
A parley ensues, and a bargain is made,
Then onward she goes like a battering ram;
Holla! Make way for the girl with the pram!

She stops at the butcher's to purchase some meat,
Some ham and some lamb, then her task is complete.
She alters her course and she makes for the gate,
With the springs of her pram groaning under the weight
Of greenstuff and groceries, pickles and jam,
And homeward she travels, the girl with the pram.

Thence forward her progress is simply superb,
She pushes the bystanders onto the kerb.
The policemen she treats with a lordly disdain,
And traffic conductors may signal in vain.
She sails o'er the crossing and holds up the tram;
Viva! Her Highness; the girl with the pram!

Oh, dear little maiden, I know you are poor,
Your station is humble, your lot is obscure.
No bays or no laurels encircle your brows,
But a warm heart beats under your neat, little blouse.
In this city of glitter and tinsel and sham,
You are solid and real—and so is your pram!

And I muse to myself as I wander alone,
How much I would give just to call you my own,
To pilot me on through the highways of life,
An honest, affectionate, brave little wife.
And cynical, crusty, and old as I am
I take off my hat to the girl with the pram.

The Lame Fiddler

It stands in its place in the dusty old case
On the rack at the end of the hall.
It is long out of use and its strings have been loose
For more years than I care to recall.
The fingers are cold that played it of old,
And I'd think it a shame and a sin,
For the old fiddler's sake, if a strange hand should wake
The strains of that old violin.

He was lame, he was poor, and the coat that he wore
Was shabby and threadbare and frayed,
But his face seemed to glow when he handled the bow,
And we danced to the tunes that he played.
I can still see him there with his long, silver hair,
And his fiddle tucked under his chin,
And we swayed and we swung. Ah; it's grand to be young
To the strains of an old violin!

In the Bush long ago, with the lamps all aglow,
We hadn't a sorrow or care
When we met of a night, but it didn't seem right
Unless the old fiddler was there.
With his kindly, old face and his violin-case,
We were eager to welcome him in,
For soft as the dew were the notes that he drew
From the heart of that old violin.

He would bow with a smile in an old-fashioned style
That belonged to a courtlier day,
And the music would flow from under his bow

Whatever we asked him to play.
He knew all the airs that were played at the fairs,
And loud was the laughter and din,
But plaintive and sweet o'er the shuffle of feet
Rose the strains of the old violin.

Our sweethearts and wives had the time of their lives,
And they joined in the merriment too,
For the women and men were more jovial then,
And their hearts were more loyal and true.
I was dancing one night with a girl fair and slight
Whose heart I was eager to win.
I asked her to wed, and she nodded her head
To the tune of that old violin.

When the old fiddler died I was called to his side,
His breathing was laboured and low,
But a smile crossed his face when I opened the case
And gave him the fiddle and bow.
He held it caressed like a babe to his breast
With his fingers so shrunken and thin.
"I'm dying," he said, as I bent o'er the bed,
And he gave me his old violin.

But the years have rolled on, and my youth has long gone,
And the fiddle is all that remains
To recall the delights of those far-away nights
When I danced to its silvery strains.
But a glory still clings round its silent, old strings,
And I'd think it a shame and a sin
If ever I sold, for silver or gold,
My keepsake—the old violin!

The Last of the Kellys

So the life of Jim Kelly has ended at last,
>And a link has been snapped with the picturesque past;

He has mounted and ridden away to the west,
>In search of a place of contentment and rest,

And I feel in my heart that an era is dead,
>With the last of the Kellys, the brother of Ned.

Mayhap he has heard, from the heart of the range,
>A faraway cooee insistent and strange,

Falling familiar, yet faint, on his ears,
>A cry that he knew in the far distant years

When the day was far spent, and the ranges were red—
>The call of his brothers, Dan Kelly and Ned.

At this distance of time it is easy to blame,
>But none can deny that the Kellys were game;

They were reckless and wild as the horses they rode,
>But a certain stern chivalry softened their code.

Now, faint as the hoofbeats of faraway steeds
>In the ranges at night, is the fame of their deeds.

As to what was the reason or whose was the guilt
   Of the lives that were lost and the blood that was spilt,
More than enough has already been said;
   The curtain has fallen, the actors are dead.
But over the ranges, in story and song,
   The wild Kelly horsemen still thunder along.

So vale Jim Kelly, the last of them all,
   And the last of the Kellys to answer the call;
The curlews and plovers have sounded his knell,
   And the night winds are sighing a mournful farewell.
May the warm rains of Autumn fall soft on the bed
   Of Kelly, Jim Kelly, the brother of Ned.

Lords of the Weddin Range

Rattle of hoofs on the mountain road
    When the naked moon rides high,
And the settler hears from his lone abode
    The outlaw gang go by;
He draws the shutters and snuffs the light
    And sees that the doors are barred,
For devil's work is afoot to-night
    When Hall and his gang ride hard.

A lantern swings by the shanty door,
    And its shadowy light is cast
A moment's space on the gang—no more—
    As the riders thunder past.
The law may watch on the plains beneath;
    It's little the outlaws care,
When spurred and booted and armed to the teeth
    They break from their mountain lair.

In the dead of the night their hoofbeats drum
    On the road through the foothills low;
The wakened settlers hear them come
    And the settlers hear them go.
They breathe a sigh as the gang goes by,
    Fearless and fierce and strange,
For none may challenge, or none deny
    The Lords of the Weddin Range.

A glare is seen in the western skies;
    The troopers are riding hard
To a home on the plains, where a dead man lies
    Face up in the station yard.
There's a smouldering heap where the haystack stood,
    The stables are burning still;
And the dead man lies in a pool of blood,
    As the dawn breaks cold and chill.

Oh, it's many a year since the ranges rang
    To the hoofs of the outlaws' steeds,
But the bold Ben Hall and his reckless gang
    Live on in their lawless deeds.
And still, they say, on the Weddin Range,
    When the naked moon rides high,
And the curlews are crying aloof and strange,
    Ben Hall and his gang go by.

The Ghost of Ben Hall

In a bend where the Lachlan flows peacefully on
    It stands in a clump of belars,
A tumble-down relic of days that are gone,
    It dreams 'neath the light of the stars;
It is tenanted now by the owls and the bats
    And they fly in and out through the door.
But big bearded bushmen in cabbage-tree hats
    Ride up to the shanty no more.

What tales it could tell, if its walls had a tongue,
    Of its lurid and reprobate past;
Of the jokes that were played and the songs that were sung
    When the gin and the whisky flowed fast.
A hard drinking lot were those bushman of old,
    And they gathered from near and from far.
But all of the riders lie under the mould
    Who drank in that tumble-down bar.

Ben Hall often sampled its whisky and gin
    When he came to the bend with his gang,
And the walls and the rafters rang loud to the din
    Of the boisterous songs that they sang.
Ben Hall was a troublesome person at times
    But he paid like a man for his grog,
And he paid in full measure at last for his crimes
    For the police shot him down like a dog.

But time is a tyrant, and time travels fast,
    And the old shanty stands in the shade,
And mourns for the men of the picturesque past
    And the jokes and the antics they played.
The curlews lament from the rushes and reeds
    When the shadows of evening descend;
But big bearded bushmen on half-broken steeds
    Come riding no more to the bend.

But the old hands declare that on cold winter nights,
    When the heavens are misty and blurred,
The shanty is filled with mysterious lights
    And voices and laughter are heard.
And they say you can see, when the door swings ajar,
    A figure, black-bearded and tall,
Revolver in hand, by the side of the bar—
    And they swear it's the Ghost of Ben Hall.

Morgan

When Morgan crossed the Murray to Peechelba and doom
A sombre silent shadow rode with him through the gloom.
The wild things of the forest slunk from the outlaw's track,
The boobook croaked a warning, "Go back, go back, go back!"
It woke no answering echo in Morgan's blackened soul,
As onward through the darkness he rode towards his goal.

An evil man was Morgan, a price was on his head;
The simple bush-folk whispered his very name with dread;
Before the fierce Dan Morgan, the bravest man might quake—
A cold and callous killer, he killed for killing's sake.
Past swamp and creek and gully, and settler's lone abode,
Towards the station homestead the grim Dan Morgan rode.

And still that hooded horseman that Morgan could not see,
Watched by the wild bush-creatures, rode close beside his knee.
Before them in a clearing a drover's campfire burned:
The phantom rode with Morgan, and turned when Morgan turned.
And loud the boobook's warning came on the cold night air,
"Go back, go back, Dan Morgan. Beware, beware, beware!"

He reached the station homestead; into the hall he strode,
And on his evil features the flickering lamplight glowed.
"Into one room!" he thundered. "Bring me a glass of grog!
If any disobey me, I'll shoot him like a dog!"
With pistols cocked and ready, dark-eyed and beetle-browed—
Before the famous outlaw the bravest hearts were cowed.

All night with loaded pistols he dozed and muttered there,
All night the evil shadow stood close beside his chair.
The brave Scotch girl McDonald, a lass who knew no fear,
Slipped out unseen by Morgan to warn the homesteads near.
And in the hours of darkness, before the break of dawn,
Around the fierce Dan Morgan the fatal net was drawn.

Day broke upon the Murray, the morning mists were gone,
The magpies sang their matins, the river murmured on.
When Morgan left the homestead and neared the stockyard gate
He heard the boobook's warning, and turned, but turned too late—
For Quinlan pressed the trigger as Morgan swung around,
And sent the grim bushranger blaspheming to the ground.

So fell the dread Dan Morgan in eighteen sixty-five,
In death as much unpitied as hated when alive.
He lived by blood and plunder, an outlaw to the end;
In life he showed no mercy, in death he left no friend.
And all who seek to follow in Morgan's evil track
Should heed the boobook's warning: "Go back, go back, go back!"

Guinan

Across the wind-swept Mallee lands, the light of sunset
    glowed
As Guinan humped his heavy swag along the river road;
His bearded face was set and grim, with every breath he
    drew,
It seemed the old wound in his side was opened up anew.

An old slouch hat was on his head, beneath whose tattered
    brim,
He gazed towards the setting sun with sunken eyes and dim;
Despair and bitter self-contempt were stamped upon his
    brow,
For Guinan's buoyancy and youth were gone for ever now.

He reached his camping ground at last, the bend was hushed
    and still,
But Guinan did not light a fire, he felt too weak and ill.
He sighed and laid his weary limbs beside a gum's green boll,
And fought to curb the bitter thoughts that sear the
    drunkard's soul.

And as the shades of evening sank to silence more profound,
Strange fancies rose to Guinan's mind from memory's burial
    ground.
Far off he heard the curlews wail, a sad and lonely cry,
And in the darkness close at hand the river rolling by.

A drowsy feeling o'er him stole, he heard, or thought he
    heard,
Familiar voices from the past in every leaf that stirred.
Across his haggard, upturned face, a ray of moonlight
    crept—
And Guinan sank into a dream, and knew not that he slept.

He dreamed that he was young once more, a youth lithe-
    limbed and brown,
As he had been long years ago ere drink had got him down,
When light of heart he rolled his swag, and roamed the bush
    for years,
Where few were better with their fists, or faster with the
    shears.

He lived his whole life o'er again, he saw with no surprise
Familiar scenes go drifting past before his dreaming eyes:
The dances in the old bush homes, where couples laughed
    and swung,
The roving days, the droving days, when all the world was
    young.

And then there came a poignant scene. It was a Queensland
    town;
A slender girl before him stood, with pleading eyes of brown.
He saw the sorrow in her face, he knew he was to blame
But Guinan rolled his swag that night, and left her to her
    shame.

Then other scenes succeeded fast: a transport far at sea,
The moonlit decks, the tropic nights, the camaraderie,
The harbor lights of foreign ports, a camp beside the Nile,
The strange, veiled women of the East, dark eyed and full of guile.

But there were other, darker scenes; in many a foreign den
He saw the base and loathsome things that mar the souls of men.
And Guinan knew, deep in his soul, whatever went or came,
To him the careless old bush life would never be the same.

And then grim scenes of battle rose, he saw his comrades die,
He felt the ice-cold clutch of fear as death went snarling by.
There was no mercy on the earth, nor mercy in the sky.
He heard men curse, he heard them pray, he saw them fight and fall.
He saw them fling their lives away at mateship's sacred call.
He saw man's splendid spirit rise triumphant over all.

The bloody shambles of Lone Pine, the trenches filled with dead,
His comrades lying stark and cold, their tunics splashed and red;
He stood beside their open graves with mates tight-lipped and stern,
And deep within his soul he felt a dull resentment burn.

The desert fight began at dawn, and rolled o'er ridge and hill,
And now with darkness close at hand the day was doubtful still.
A lurid cloud of dust and smoke hung o'er the dreary scene,
And far around the dead lay strewn in wadi and ravine;

When high upon a windswept hill that overlooked the field,
Outlined against the setting sun, a line of horsemen wheeled;
A gust of shrapnel swept the ridge, the heavens turned to flame,
And roaring from the setting sun, a red tornado came.

A breathing space, the squadrons poised, then swept to the attack;
They needed neither spur nor goad on that grim battle-track.
Stern leaders watched the battle cloud close o'er the brown brigade.
The sands of time were running low, Chauvel's last card was played.

With bayonets bared the bush brigades went thundering down the steep;
The 5.9's went roaring by, the Moslem lead bit deep.
But high above the sound of guns and shrapnel whistling shrill,
The thunder of those steel-shod hoofs rolled over ridge and hill.

And Guinan knew like all who rode in that fierce cavalcade,
Defeat or victory rested now on one lone bush brigade.
They swept across the rifle pits, they neared the blazing town—
A bullet went through Guinan's hat; his section mate went down.
Then came a sudden blinding flash, a searing stab of pain;
The rifle dropped from Guinan's hand, he lost his bridle rein.
A blood red mist was in his eyes, a numbness in his brain.
He heard the thundering beat of hoofs grow faint and far away,
As on Beersheba's shot-lashed ridge beside his horse he lay.
A shudder shook the sleeping man, his face grew ashen grey.

So Guinan slept to wake no more, his dream had reached its end,
And deeper still the silence fell in that lone river bend.
A shadow passed across the moon, a sable pinioned bird,
Brushed close to Guinan's upturned cheek, but Guinan never stirred.

The daylight broadened in the east, the stars grew faint and few,
And through the lofty Murray gums the winds of dawning blew;
The magpies sang their morning songs, a flock of gay galahs
Went screaming down the river bank among the green belars.
A dead man lay beneath the trees, his face upturned and wan;
And in the early morning light, the Murray murmured on.

Insomnia

There's something wrong with my brain to-night,
 Though I've drawn the blinds and I've snuffed the light.
I can't, for the life of me, sleep a wink,
 But I lie in the dark, and I think and think
While the hours creep by and the clock ticks loud
 Like the steady tramp of a marching crowd.
And the forms and the faces of men long dead
 Peer and chuckle around my bed.
I watch them come and I watch them go
 And they nudge each other and whistle low
Though the doors are locked and the windows too.
 Now, what the hell is a man to do?

Hello, Curran, you damned old scamp,
 First of the mates that I met in camp.
If I had a bottle, we'd drink a toast,
 To old Romani and Terry's post.
But I know you are only an empty ghost.
 When last we met we were far away—
That was at Raffa one scorching day;
 It was Christmas time, but we had no spread,
Only bullets and bombs instead;
 And in lieu of whisky and beers and wines,
A gust of shrapnel and five point nines—
 Christmas cheer from the Moslem lines.

We had marched all night, we were parched with thirst;
    So were our horses, and how we cursed
As we swung in line for the last attack,
    But we stormed their trenches and drove them back,
And I saw you later, spread-eagled out,
    Face up, in front of the first redoubt,
With most of your brains in your old slouch hat—
    But what's the good of a dream like that?

"Heads a fiver: who's got the kip?"
    "Shamrock Ryan, you take my tip!"
He'll head 'em once and he'll head 'em twice—
    He's just the same with the cards and dice:
Don't set the centre, that's my advice.
    He might do five or he might do ten—
Up they go, and they're heads again.
    Always smiling and always cool,
He won't let up till he breaks the school.
    "Fifty he heads 'em. Who wants a bet?"
"Fair go, spinner! The centre's set!"
    "And he's done another—I knew he would!"
He was always lucky, but what's the good,
    Lying there with his face all wan,
One leg shattered and one arm gone,
    While his heart is pumping his life blood out
Like water poured from a broken spout,
    And he draws his breath with a gurgling hiss—
But what's the good of a dream like this?

Night and noise in a Cairo den,
>   Half-clad women and drunken men,
A strange, burnt smell like a sacrifice
>   Offered up to the gods of vice;
Someone fumbling the broken keys
>   Of an old piano with windy wheeze—
An oath, a scuffle, a crash, a yell—
>   Drink and women don't mix too well.
"Make for the stairway! Grab that stool!
>   What's gone wrong with the drunken fool?
The jacks are coming. Put out the lights!
>   I'm sick to death with these brawls and fights!"
Crash of furniture, oaths and screams—
>   But what's the good of those ugly dreams.

Take me somewhere and sink me deep
>   Into a fathomless gulf of sleep,
With sealed up eyes and padlocked ears,
>   And let me slumber for years and years
With nothing to think of, or hear, or see:
>   That will be heaven enough for me.
I want no angels or jasper throne,
>   I only want to be left alone;
I'm sick to death with lying awake
>   Waiting and watching for day to break,
While the hours creep by, and I hear them strike,
>   Till I've almost forgotten what sleep is like;
And the ghostly figures that haunt the gloom
>   Peer and chuckle about the room
Till dawn's cold light on the window gleams
>   And puts an end to those ugly dreams.

Brunette and Blonde

Oh, the little brunette is a gay coquette,
    And so is the blue eyed blonde;
It's little they care if the skies are fair,
    Or lovers be false or fond.
The world may smile or the world may frown,
    It's little they reck or rue—
The little brunette with the eyes of brown
    And the blonde with the eyes of blue.

I love them both, and I'm rather loath
    To say whom I most prefer,
For the little brunette is a gay coquette
    And the blonde is as bad as her.
They go their way and they have their day,
    Nor worry what waits beyond—
The little brunette with the hair of jet
    And the dear little blue-eyed blonde.

Oh, little brunette, your eyes are wet
    And heavy with tears unshed;
You were always fond of your sister blonde—
    Now the dear little blonde is wed.
For the cupid laughed as he drew the shaft,
    And the little blind god aimed true,
And he lodged the dart in the yielding heart
    Of the blonde with the eyes of blue.

But, little brunette, you need not fret
    Or mourn for a broken bond,
For soon or late you will share the fate
    Of the dear little blue eyed blonde.
Though they say he's blind, you'll always find
    That the little love god aims true
When his bow is set on a gay brunette
    Or a blonde with eyes of blue.

Blood on the Rose

The Tressider mansion is brilliant to-night
    And the dancers are footing it lissome and light.
Through the big open windows the melody flows,
    Where there's blood on the lily and blood on the rose.

They swing and they sway to a dreamy old tune,
    But out in the garden, face up to the moon,
Two lovers are lying, and nobody knows
    That there's blood on the lily and blood on the rose.

Oh, the world may upbraid and the world may condemn,
    But music and laughter have ended for them.
This is the altar and bed that they chose,
    There is blood on the lily and blood on the rose.

This is their answer to gibe and to sneer,
    This is the triumph of love over fear.
Little they care now for friends or for foes,
    For there's blood on the lily and blood on the rose.

Love may absolve them and death may atone!
    Turn from their marriage bed, leave them alone,
Let the night cover what dawn will disclose,
    For there's blood on the lily and blood on the rose.

"Gentlemen, the Press!"

We've toasted all the Royal House, and all our loyal friends;
There's only one more toast, my lads, before the evening
 ends.
We've had a rather merry time, I think you will agree.
Now, to propose the final toast, the Chairman calls on me.
So charge your glasses, gentlemen; I have the happiness
And honour to propose the toast of 'Gentlemen, the Press.'

So pause a moment, if you please, I have a word to say
About our free, enlightened press, the papers of to-day.
Should any member of the press be present here to-night,
I hope that he will mark my word and get my meaning
 right;
I will not keep you long, I hope—it's nothing more or less
Than my opinion of the toast of "Gentlemen, the Press".

Well, what the devil is the press—perhaps my words are
 rude—
But tell me what it ever did to earn our gratitude?
It's always on the rich man's side; it makes my blood run
 cold
To think of all the harm it's done and all the lies it's told.
It never tries to bring reform or mitigate distress;
It fools the people all the time, the bitter Tory press.

When times are bad, and work is scarce, and hunger stalks the town,
The press is always to the fore to drag the worker down.
They talk about production costs and other played-out gags—
But always charge the same old price for their disastrous rags.
They never try to lend a hand when things are in a mess;
They're barren of constructive thought, the helpless, whining press.

But when election time comes round, they're out to save the state
(You'll always find them ranged behind the wealthy candidate).
They deal out doleful prophecies of woe that will ensue
Should Labor chance to gain the day and push its programme through.
They have a dread of Labor rule; how earnestly they stress
The danger to the Commonwealth—the grave, impartial press.

But should a Royal visitor arrive from overseas
You'll find the press is always there to greet him—on their knees.
How earnestly they note his words, how gallantly they vie
To prove their patriotic zeal beneath the Royal eye.
I'd like some travelling Duke or Prince to candidly confess
His honest, true opinion of the sycophantic press.

Should rumours of a Royal birth go round, the press will strive
To be close handy to the spot, to see the child arrive.
And if they don't succeed in this, the christening finds them there
To note the infant's Royal nose, the colour of its hair.
And should a Prince or Princess wed, they're always there to bless
The nuptials of the Royal pair, the noble-hearted press.

The racing season sees them shine; they're always on the lawn
To watch the ladies tripping by in coats of beige and fawn.
They like to be on speaking terms with Lady This or That—
But never deign to cast a glance across the common Flat.
Poor workless girls may tramp the streets to sell a cheap caress—
It doesn't worry them at all, the apathetic press.

Well, that's the finish, gentlemen. I think you will admit
That I've done credit to the toast—it's eased my mind a bit.
On some occasion such as this, we'll meet again, maybe,
And if you want a toast proposed, I hope you call on me.
Just one more word before I close: deep in some dark recess
I'd like to kick for good and all the whole confounded press.

The Swaggless Swaggie

This happened many years ago
    Before the bush was cleared,
When every man was six foot high
    And wore a flowing beard.
One very hot and windy day,
    Along the old coach road,
Towards Joe Murphy's halfway house
    A bearded bushman strode.

He was a huge and heavy man,
    Well over six foot high,
An old slouch hat was on his head,
    And murder in his eye.
No billycan was in his hand,
    No heavy swag he bore,
But deep and awful were the oaths
    That swagless swaggie swore.

At last he reached the shanty door.
    Into the bar he burst.
He dumped his hat upon the floor,
    And cursed and cursed and cursed.
A neighboring shed had just cut out;
    The bar was nearly full
Of shearers and of bullockies

Who'd come to cast the wool.
They were a rough and ready lot,
  The bushmen gathered there,
But every man was stricken dumb,
  To hear the stranger swear.
He cursed the bush, he cursed mankind,
  The whole wide universe.
It froze their very blood to hear
  That swagless swaggie curse.

Joe Murphy seized an empty pot
  And filled it brimming full.
The stranger raised it to his lips
  And took a mighty pull.
This seemed to cool him down a bit;
  He finished off the ale,
And to the crowd around the bar
  He told his awful tale.

"I met the Ben Hall gang," he said,
  "The blankards stuck me up!
They pinched me billy, pinched me swag,
  They pinched me flamin' pup!
They turned me pockets inside out,
  And took me only quid!
I never thought they'd pinch me pipe—
  But swelp me gawd they did!

"I spoke to 'em as man to man,
    I said I'd fight 'em all;
I would have broke O'Meally's neck,
    And tanned the hide of Hall.
They only laughed, and said good-bye,
    And rode away to brag
Of how they stuck a swaggie up,
    And robbed him of his swag.

"I never done 'em any harm,
    I thought 'em decent chaps.
But now I wouldn't raise a hand,
    To save 'em from the traps.
I'm finished with the bush for good,
    I'm off to Wagga town
Where they won't stick a swaggie up
    Or take a swaggie down."

The bushmen were a decent lot,
    As bushmen mostly are.
They filled the stranger up with beer;
    The hat went round the bar.
The shearers threw some blankets in
    To make another swag,
The rousers gave a billy can
    And brand new tucker bag;

Joe Murphy gave a meerschaum pipe
    He hadn't smoked for years.
The stranger was too full of words,
    His eyes were dim with tears.
The ringer shouted drinks all round
    And then, to top it up,
The babbling brook, the shearers' cook,
    Gave him a kelpie pup.

Next day, an hour before the dawn,
    The stranger took the track
Complete with pup and billycan,
    His swag upon his back.
Along the most forsaken roads,
    Intent on dodging graft,
He headed for the Great North West,
    And laughed, and laughed, and laughed.

Spooks and Spirits

The beer, the good old amber beer, is just the drink for me,
I never touch the harder stuff when I go on the spree,
My mates they go for other drinks, gin, brandy, rum and wine,
But while the pumps are working well the beer will do for mine.

I've always loved the amber ale since I was just a kid,
I only touched the stronger stuff but once, by George I did.
So fill your glasses up again, I'll tell you all about
The night I took the Spirits in to keep the Spirits out.

I once lived in a haunted house where spirits rapped the door
And every spook this side of Hell went marching down the floor.
I didn't worry overmuch because at first you see
I reckoned spirits had their rights the same as you and me.

But what with tramping on the stairs and knocking on the wall,
I couldn't get a wink of sleep, I got no rest at all,
So I decided there and then I'd put 'em all to rout
The night I took the Spirits in to keep the Spirits out.

I said that something must be done, it could not be endured.
Them spirits must be taught their place, their nasty habits cured.
For though I'm just a peaceful chap, a quiet sort of bloke,
Them spirits kicked up such a row, it got beyond a joke.

The pub was just across the road, the barman's name was Bill,
A very decent sort of chap who never touched the till,
I whispered something in his ear and he winked back at me;
He poured me out a double Scotch and I got on the spree.

Yes, I got on the spree all right, I went clean round the bar,
Gin, whisky, burgundy and rum and Hennessy's Three Star.
By jove, it was a mighty spree, I had a glass of hock.
Thinks I: "Now if them spirits come, I'll give 'em all a shock."

I had another double Scotch and then eased up a bit,
'Twas getting close to closing time and I was fighting fit.
I had another gin and rum and finished up on stout.
The night I took the Spirits in to keep the Spirits out.

Then back into my room I went, I had a swig of rum,
And then I had some gin and stout and in the spirits come.
I'd done some fighting in my time and learned to use my dooks
But though I'd tackled twelve stone men, I'd never fought with spooks.

They came at me from every side, all in and no holds barred.
It was a decent sot of scrap, I whacked 'em good and hard.
It was the greatest fight I'd fought since my first opening bout
The night I took the Spirits in to keep the Spirits out.

I gave them everything I had, I knocked 'em through the wall,
And then the big boss spook comes in, the greatest of them all.
He was a tall and hefty spook, clean mad and full of fight,
He swung a wicked left at me, I countered with me right.

And then I caught him on the jaw, it was a mighty clout.
It knocked him right clean through the door, the master spook was out.
I had no trouble after that, I was a bit too rough,
They never worried me again, them spooks had had enough.

So if you're asking my advice, I'd say without a doubt,
You've got to take some Spirits in to keep the Spirits out.

Brady

A bitter wind blew out of the north, and the skies were dull
>and grey,
When, spreading swiftly, the news went forth that Brady
>had passed away.
And in many a hut and miner's shack and in many a
>shearing shed
The men who toil in the great outback mourned for an old
>mate dead.

For Brady was ever a restless soul, a rover by land and sea;
He saw life clearly and saw it whole, and a minstrel born was
>he.
He loved the bush and the open plains, the light of the
>western stars,
The clink-clink-clink of the hobble-chains and the wind in
>the green belars.

He sang of the woods and the wilderness, he sang of the
>Spanish Main,
Of the gallant sailors of good Queen Bess who harried the
>ships of Spain,
Of the clipper-ships of the Indian trade, running the Easters
>down
With every inch of canvas spread, hell-bent for London
>town.

Back in the long-departed years, a spirit of vague unrest
Stirred in the hearts of the pioneers from east to the farthest
    west.
The first faint flicker of nationhood, a vision of things to be,
A mighty nation—one faith, one blood—united from sea to
    sea.

Then Lawson, Brady and Quinn betimes, united to wield
    the pen,
To tell the tales in their stirring rhymes of the hopes and the
    fears of men;
Quinn and Lawson have long since passed with the task of
    their lives fulfilled.
Now Brady follows with faith held fast in the nation he
    helped to build.

He has launched his barque on a timeless sea, to follow a
    guiding star;
He has heard from the bourne of eternity the call of his
    mate afar.
When he comes to the end of his last long quest, may the
    beacons brightly burn,
And his roving spirit at last find rest in the port of
    No Return.

Mallacoota

To the shores of Mallacoota,
    Feeling heartsick and depressed
From the tumult of the city,
    I arrived, a stranger guest.
Kindly hearts were there to greet me,
    Friendly voices welcomed me
In the house above the inlet,
    Looking o'er the sunlit sea.

On the shores of Mallacoota,
    Where the billows shoreward roll,
I have found a balm and solace
    For my overburdened soul.
For the glory of the morning
    And the splendour of the eve
Has enchanted me and chained me
    And has made me loath to leave.

Mallacoota in the moonlight
    Has a glory all its own
When the mighty sea is muttering
    In a muffled undertone;
And when rain is on the waters
    And the heavens give no light,
Then the light from mighty Gabo
    Like a great sword cleaves the night.

I have always loved the forest,
>   I have always loved the sea;
Now here at Mallacoota
>   Both my loves are close to me.
I can feel their mighty pulses,
>   I can hear their great hearts beat
With the forest close behind me
>   And the ocean at my feet.

We are all a part of nature,
>   Part of what we feel and see,
And I feel that Mallacoota
>   Has become a part of me.
And wherever I may wander,
>   Or whatever beacons burn,
To the shores of Mallacoota
>   I will once again return.

Winds of the Wilderness

I have wandered in many places,
    I have eaten my bread with tears;
Many and strange are the faces
    I have met in the winged years.
But now I am old and weary,
    I drift on my way in pain—
Oh, winds of the wilderness, bear me
    Back to my home again.

Dazzled by dream alluring,
    Eager the world to roam,
I severed life's golden mooring
    And steered from the lights of home.
Now, far from the hearts that love me,
    And far from my native shore,
Dark are the skies above me,
    Stormy the seas before.

Oft in the night-time lonely
    I see the homelight gleam.
Waking, I find it only
    A will-o'-the-wisp—a dream.
Chalice of life, I have quaffed thee,
    Only the dregs remain—
Oh, winds of the wilderness, waft me
    Back to my home again.

Ballad of Discontent

Oh, this is a ballad of discontent,
    Sung in a minor key,
Like the desolate curlews' far lament,
    Or the moan of the distant sea;
A song of sorrow for days long done,
    Ere science arose to mar
The dreams of man, and the blazing sun
    Was God in a golden car;
When Sappho flourished, and Homer sang,
    To the glory of God and man—
Oh, the world was merry, the world was young,
    And danced to the pipes of Pan.

But Pan and Homer are dead, and faint
    Is the echo of pagan glee;
A gloom of heaviness seems to taint,
    The splendours of earth and sea.
We have felled the forest and marred the stream
    Where the shy nymphs loved to hide;
We have laid rude hands on the pagan dreams,
    And riven their veils aside.
We dance no more in the moonlit glade,
    Where magic and music blent;
Our souls are fettered by bonds of trade,
    And burdened by discontent.

There is war in the east, and war in the west,
    And the days are dark ahead;
The world is filled with a fierce unrest,
    And heavy with doubt and dread.
There is death in the air, and death on the sea,
    And death on the shell-torn sod,
While the great guns bellow with gusty glee,
    Their blasphemous song to God.
As I gaze around on a world gone mad,
    My sorrow must find a vent.
Do you wonder then that my song is sad
    And heavy with discontent?

The sun shines bright in the early morn,
    And the ocean's breast is fair,
But the caves are empty, the rocks forlorn,
    Where the mermaids combed their hair.
They sport no more in the seaways green,
    As they did in the olden time;
But a loathsome brood in the depths unseen
    Lie crouched in the weed and slime,
And the great ship reels with her bulkheads torn,
    And her steel ribs gashed and rent,
While her maddened bellow is landward borne
    The cry of her discontent.

Little quarter of old they gave,
   At the fall of a leagured town—
But who can succour to-day, or save,
   When the bombs come whirling down?
It is woe alike to the strong and weak,
   To the women and children woe,
In the dead of night when the sirens shriek
   And the warbirds circle low.
Blazing cities and shell-torn fields,
   Where the dead lie heaped and pent—
Is this the harvest our wisdom yields,
   The fruits of our discontent?

We have probed the planets and weighed the sun,
   We have girdled the sea and earth,
But what is the measure of all we've done
   And what are our conquests worth?
Is man less prone to the evil thought?
   Less given to evil deeds?
Or do we live in a world distraught
   In a welter of warring creeds?
We can only wait for the storm to cease,
   And pray when its rage is spent,
That the sun will rise on a world at peace,
   Unburdened with discontent.

End of a Joyous Bard

The poor old bard is dead at last,
    There's grief in all the city—
He didn't even say good-bye,
    Or write a farewell ditty.
We found a partly finished ode
    Amongst his private papers,
Wedged in between two unpaid bills,
    The grocer's and the draper's.

And so he's bade the world farewell,
    And left us all the poorer.
The tailors, too, they'll mourn for him—
    Of that there's nothing surer.
The city bars won't seem the same,
    There's no one to replace him.
He's gone where critics cannot scoff,
    Or debt collectors chase him.

He was an optimistic bard,
    And moderately sober;
And many a time, when short of cash,
    He drank great draughts of Robur.
But with a few convivial friends,
    He really could be merry.
He always saw he got his share
    Of brandy, beer and sherry.

'Twas grand to see him in a bar,
> A picture of decorum,
A look of wisdom on his face,
> A pot of beer before him,
Monopolising all the talk—
> Unless when some one shouted—
He never paid for one himself,
> He made no bones about it.

His politics were somewhat broad,
> His morals rather broader;
He didn't hold with Parliaments,
> And laughed at law and order.
He had a grudge against the force,
> He'd lift no hand to save them—
They ran the poet in one night;
> He never quite forgave them.

He was a Socialist at heart,
> He called all men his brothers.
Excepting certain editors
> And creditors and others.
He held all critics in contempt,
> For, in his own opinion,
He equalled Masefield at his best,
> And had the call on Binyon.

The going wasn't always good—
> He struck some nasty patches,
And levied toll upon his friends
> For cigarettes and matches,

He was a master of the art,
    The gentle art of "humming",
And always made his victims think,
    A cheque would soon be coming.

He got a good bit out of life,
    But certain things annoyed him:
He had to tell his friends himself
    How much the world enjoyed him;
And if you met him out of sorts,
    Ill-tempered and dejected,
You thought of Sherlock Holmes and said:
    "H'm, Watson ... H'm, rejected."

He kept his balance fairly well,
    Except in certain seasons;
He never got completely drunk,
    Except for proper reasons—
A birthday or a funeral;
    And on those rare occasions
He suffered very little harm,
    Except a few abrasions.

And now he's gone, the Lord knows where,
    And left us all behind him.
I hope the angels treat him fair—
    That is, if they can find him.
I wish the Lord had let him stay,
    To finish off his "poem";
But here he lies, a poet mourned
    By those who didn't know him.

Requiem

Now is the long day ended,
　　Now is my journey done.
Shadows royal and splendid
　　Gather around the sun.
What have I broken or mended,
　　What have I lost or won?

Foolish and fruitless query,
　　What does it signify?
Night winds, fitful and eerie,
　　Tell me the end is nigh.
I am too old and weary,
　　To ponder the how and the why.

What does it really matter,
　　What does life really mean?
Shadows and idle chatter
　　Thrown on an empty screen.
Whatever we sow or scatter,
　　It's little enough we glean.

Many must meet their ending
 On fields where the great guns rave.
Others as brave, contending,
 Sink in the lone night wave.
And some with a few friends bending
 Over an open grave.

But whether sooner or later,
 In the dry leaf or the green,
The lover as well as the hater,
 The soiled as well as the clean,
Must bow to the great dictator
 Whose sword is always keen.

Life is a counterfeiter,
 A rogue; though his wares entice
In youth, when our taste is sweeter,
 We buy, but we pay the price.
For life is a mighty cheater
 And he plays with a loaded dice.

But who, when the light is failing
 And the pleasures of youth have cloyed,
Will answer the doubts assailing
 A soul by a faith unbuoyed
Only the wild winds wailing
 Far out in the darkening void.

Acknowledgements

This book would not have been possible without the generous support and encouragement of many people.

I am deeply grateful to Carmen, Isabel and Dianne for their unwavering support.

My sincere thanks go to Hilary Reynolds for her proofreading, and to Sandra Nobes for her design work and support. Thanks to Erica Wagner and Andrea McNamara for their thoughtful advice and encouragement.

I am particularly indebted to Philip Mead, whose scholarly expertise and passion for Australian literature were instrumental in bringing this project to fruition.

To librarians everywhere, especially the dedicated staff at the State Library of Victoria, I extend my heartfelt appreciation for years of patient assistance, support and encouragement. Your commitment to preserving and sharing our literary heritage makes work like this possible.

Finally, to my colleagues and the brilliant students at Nagle Catholic College, Bairnsdale—thank you for your enthusiasm and for reminding me daily why literature matters. Let your light shine.

www.ingramcontent.com/pod-product-compliance
Lightning Source LLC
Chambersburg PA
CBHW020106240426
43661CB00002B/54